TABLE OF CONTENTS

Introduction — 01

Chapter 1: Understanding the Digital Marketing Landscape — 03

Chapter 2: Setting Up for Success — 11

Chapter 3: Developing a Content Strategy — 57

Chapter 4: Using customer journey mapping to refine marketing efforts — 74

Chapter 5: Building a Scalable Digital Marketing Ecosystem — 91

Conclusion — 101

WWW.JUSTMARKETINGINSIGHTS.COM

INTRODUCTION

WELCOME TO THE ESSENTIAL PLAYBOOK OF DIGITAL MARKETING FUNDAMENTALS

In this digital era, where commerce and conversation alike have moved online, mastering digital marketing is no longer just an advantage - it's a necessity. This eBook, "Digital Marketing 101: Essentials' Playbook," is your gateway to understanding and harnessing the power of digital marketing. Whether you are an entrepreneur, a business owner eager to expand your digital footprint, or a marketer looking to refine your skills, this guide is designed to equip you with the foundational knowledge and practical strategies needed for success in the digital world.

The primary purpose of this eBook is to demystify the core concepts of digital marketing and provide you with the tools to implement effective digital strategies. We aim to bridge the gap between novice enthusiasm and expert insight, making sophisticated marketing techniques accessible and actionable for everyone. This guide serves as the cornerstone of a series that will delve deeper into specific platforms and advanced tactics, setting a solid groundwork on which you can build and expand.

INTRODUCTION

WHAT IS DIGITAL MARKETING?

Digital marketing encompasses all marketing efforts that use an electronic device or the internet. Businesses leverage digital channels such as search engines, social media, email, and other websites to connect with current and prospective customers. Unlike traditional marketing, digital marketing offers unprecedented levels of interaction and engagement with audiences, measurable in real-time and highly adaptable to the evolving preferences of consumers.

IMPORTANCE OF DIGITAL MARKETING IN THE MODERN BUSINESS LANDSCAPE

In today's fast-paced, digital-first world, traditional marketing techniques alone are insufficient to achieve business growth and consumer connection. Digital marketing not only allows businesses to reach a larger audience but also enables them to target the consumers most likely to buy their products or services. It provides measurable analytics that can improve the effectiveness of marketing strategies and increase the return on investment. Furthermore, digital marketing levels the playing field, allowing smaller businesses the chance to compete against bigger players and attract a global audience.

It is important to keep in mind that the landscape of digital marketing is ever-evolving. Staying updated with the latest trends and continually adapting your strategies will be key to maintaining relevance and achieving sustained success.

CHAPTER 1

Understanding the Digital Marketing Landscape

In the last few years, marketing has transformed from a monologue into a dynamic conversation. Digital marketing isn't just about pushing your message out into the world; it involves engaging with your audience in real-time, using a variety of platforms and strategies to achieve business and branding objectives. The beauty of digital marketing lies in its versatility and reach. It allows marketers to disseminate information across a global platform without physical limits or substantial delays.

KEY DIGITAL MARKETING CHANNELS AND THEIR ROLE

Understanding the key channels of digital marketing is essential for crafting effective strategies. Each channel serves a unique purpose and interacts with the audience in specific ways. Here's a detailed look at some of the most important digital marketing channels and what they offer to marketers.

1. Search Engines

Role: Search engines are the pillars of digital visibility, acting as the gatekeepers to the Internet. They serve as the primary method for users to discover new content, products, and services. By optimizing for search engines through SEO and SEM (Search Engine Marketing), businesses can increase their visibility and credibility online.

CHAPTER 1: Understanding the Digital Marketing Landscape

Importance: High rankings in search results can drive a significant amount of organic traffic to a website, making SEO one of the most cost-effective marketing strategies. The beauty of search engines is that you don't chase clients; rather, clients chase you. When people search for a specific product or keyword associated with your products or services, they already recognize their need. They are actively seeking a solution, and with the right SEO and SEM strategies, your product or service can be that solution. This readiness to buy makes traffic from search engines extremely valuable. The ability to rank well in search results not only drives significant organic traffic to your website but also increases your brand's credibility and trustworthiness.

Strategies: To capitalize on this dynamic, it's crucial to invest in both SEO and SEM. SEO focuses on optimizing your content and website structure to appear naturally in search results, which builds long-term equity for your brand. On the other hand, SEM involves paid advertising like PPC (Pay-Per-Click), which can provide immediate visibility and results, perfect for new product launches or targeted promotions.

2. Social Media

Role: Social media platforms serve as dynamic venues for interaction and engagement, not just between friends and family, but between brands and consumers. These platforms allow for direct communication, content sharing, and community building, making them an indispensable part of modern digital marketing strategies.

WWW.JUSTMARKETINGINSIGHTS.COM

CHAPTER 1: Understanding the Digital Marketing Landscape

Importance: The power of social media lies in its capacity to foster engagement and build relationships. Brands can interact with their audience in real-time, respond to trends, gather feedback, and personalize their outreach. Unlike search engines where clients actively seek solutions, social media allows you to proactively reach out to potential customers where they spend a lot of their time. By maintaining a strong, engaging presence on appropriate social media platforms, your brand not only increases its visibility but also enhances its approachability and relatability, which are crucial for trust-building and brand loyalty. This approachable presence ensures that when customers are ready to buy, your brand is top of mind, effectively pulling them into your sales funnel.

Strategies: Content diversification: Tailor your content to the unique style and user expectations of each platform. What works on Instagram may not resonate on LinkedIn. Invest in a variety of content types, such as videos, live sessions, infographics, and user-generated content to engage different segments of your audience.

Engagement optimization: Regularly engage with your followers through comments, polls, and interactive stories. This two-way interaction enriches the user experience and boosts your visibility due to platform algorithms favoring highly interactive posts. Plus, it may help you understand your audience better.

Influencer collaborations: Partner with influencers who resonate with your target audience to extend your reach. Influencers can introduce your brand to their followers in a natural and trusted way, driving both awareness and conversion.

Understanding the Digital Marketing Landscape

Paid advertising: Utilize the sophisticated targeting options offered by social media platforms to deliver ads directly to your ideal demographic. Tailored ads can help you reach potential customers based on their interests, behaviors, and more, making your campaigns more relevant and effective.

Analytics and adjustments: Leverage the detailed analytics tools provided by social media platforms to track the performance of your posts and campaigns. Analyze this data to refine your strategy, optimize content, and improve engagement rates.

3. Email marketing

Role: Email marketing remains one of the most direct and personal forms of communication to reach an audience. Contrary to some claims, it is not dead. It actually is one of the most powerful tools you have at your fingertips. Its power lies in its precision and personalization capabilities. Through sophisticated segmentation and targeting techniques, you can tailor your messages to meet the specific interests and needs of different segments of your audience. This customization can range from disseminating general company updates to delivering highly personalized offers and products. It is important to understand that email marketing is far more than just dispatching promotional messages to a customer's inbox; it's a profound way to forge connections and enrich the lives of your audience. This channel offers the unique opportunity to share valuable insights, provide solutions, and deliver content that resonates on a personal level. A common guideline many marketers follow is the 80/20 rule. This rule suggests that 80% of your content should focus on delivering value and engaging your audience with insights, tips, and useful information, while the remaining 20% can be devoted to promotions, sales, and direct calls to action.

Understanding the Digital Marketing Landscape

Importance: With high ROI, email marketing is ideal for lead nurturing, sales conversions, and customer retention. It's a controlled medium, meaning you can carefully craft the message, timing, and audience segmentation without interference from external algorithms. It offers the unique advantage of nurturing leads through carefully designed sequences that guide potential customers along the buyer's journey, ultimately building loyalty and increasing customer lifetime value. It is an essential tool for creating an ongoing dialogue that fosters a deep, personal connection with your audience. In a world where consumers are bombarded with countless digital interactions each day, email marketing allows you to break through the noise with messages that are not only seen but felt.

Strategies: Firstly, segment your email list based on user behavior, demographics, or purchase history to deliver more relevant and personalized messages. Craft compelling subject lines that pique interest and encourage recipients to open your emails. Utilize A/B testing to determine which subject lines, content, and calls-to-action resonate best with different segments of your audience. Automate email campaigns to nurture leads systematically through welcome sequences, follow-ups on abandoned carts, and re-engagement messages.

Optimize for mobile as a significant portion of emails are opened on mobile devices, ensuring your email design is responsive and visually appealing on all screens. Finally, regularly analyze your email performance metrics to refine your approach, improve content, and better align with your audience's preferences, thereby enhancing the overall impact of your email marketing efforts.

CHAPTER 1 — Understanding the Digital Marketing Landscape

4. Content Marketing

Role: Content marketing is the backbone of digital marketing; it is found in every area of marketing because, fundamentally, everything in marketing revolves around content. Whether it's a tweet, a product description on a website, a blog post, or even a press release, each piece of information shared is content that serves a purpose. The focus shifts from selling to telling, so the role of content marketing is to shape perceptions, educate consumers, build relationships, and drive loyalty. By delivering consistently high-quality and valuable content, businesses can effectively communicate their brand story, illustrate their values, and establish themselves as thought leaders in their industry. This integral approach ensures that content marketing is not viewed as a separate or dispensable part of your marketing strategy, but as the glue that holds together various marketing initiatives.

From improving SEO to enhancing social media engagement, from nurturing leads via email to converting them through persuasive landing pages, content marketing's influence is ubiquitous and transformative.

Importance: Content marketing fundamentally enhances the customer journey and enriches the user experience at every digital touchpoint. This strategy not only supports the acquisition of new customers but also plays a pivotal role in retaining existing ones by providing continuous value. Engaging content keeps the audience informed and connected, making them more likely to stay loyal to the brand.

Moreover, content marketing significantly impacts organic search rankings and digital visibility. By consistently publishing high-quality content that resonates with the audience and answers their queries, businesses improve their SEO standings, which drives more organic traffic to their sites over time. This increased visibility not only boosts brand awareness but also enhances credibility and authority in the market.

Understanding the Digital Marketing Landscape

Additionally, content marketing offers a scalable way to generate leads and conversions without the direct costs associated with traditional advertising. By leveraging powerful calls-to-action within content, businesses can guide readers towards taking the next step in their buyer's journey, be it subscribing to a newsletter, downloading a resource, or making a purchase.
This strategic approach to driving engagement and conversion rates highlights the critical role content marketing plays in achieving long-term business goals.

Strategies: Understand your audience: Before creating content, it's crucial to have a clear understanding of your audience's needs, preferences, and pain points. Utilizing tools like buyer personas and audience segmentation can guide your content strategy and help ensure that the content you produce is relevant and engaging to those you aim to reach.

Diversify content types: To appeal to different preferences and increase engagement, diversify your content types. Consider a mix of blogs, videos, infographics, podcasts, and webinars. Each format can cater to different segments of your audience and can be used in various stages of the buyer's journey.

Focus on quality and value: Ensure that the content you produce is both high-quality and valuable. This means well-researched, well-written, and visually appealing content that addresses your audience's questions and needs. High-quality content is more likely to be consumed, shared, and linked to, which not only helps with SEO but also with building credibility.

Understanding the Digital Marketing Landscape

5. Mobile Marketing

Role: Given that most users keep their mobile devices within reach at all times, mobile marketing presents a unique opportunity for real-time engagement and personalized communication. This channel is essential for reaching consumers directly, whether they are on the go or at home, making it a critical element in modern marketing campaigns.

Importance: Mobile marketing allows businesses to reach customers at critical moments with targeted messaging based on real-time data, such as location and behavior. This immediacy and relevance enhance the effectiveness of marketing efforts and can significantly increase engagement rates.

Mobile also plays a vital role in the shopping process, from initial research to final purchase, making it indispensable for a seamless omnichannel experience. Consumers expect a consistent and smooth interaction across all platforms, and mobile marketing helps fulfill these expectations by integrating with other digital marketing channels, enhancing the overall customer journey.

Strategies: Optimize for Mobile-First: Ensure that all your digital content, especially your website and emails, are mobile-friendly. This means fast loading times, responsive design, and intuitive navigation that suits smaller screens and touch-based interactions.

Utilize SMS and MMS: Send timely and relevant information through SMS (Short Message Service) or MMS (Multimedia Messaging Service). These messages can include promotions, updates, and alerts that encourage immediate engagement or action.

Develop a Mobile App: If applicable, developing a mobile app can provide a direct marketing channel to your customers, offering them a more streamlined and personalized user experience. Use push notifications wisely to keep your users informed and engaged without overwhelming them.

CHAPTER 2

Setting Up for Success

IDENTIFYING YOUR TARGET AUDIENCE

Understanding Customer Personas

Identifying your target audience begins with the development of customer personas. These personas are semi-fictional characters that represent the ideal customers you want to attract based on real data about demographics and online behavior, along with educated speculations about their personal histories, motivations, and concerns. Creating detailed personas can help you understand not only who your audience is but also why they may be interested in what you have to offer.

For a small to medium-sized enterprise, an agreed rule of thumb in marketing is having 3 to 5 customer personas. This range is manageable yet diverse enough to cover different segments of a typical market without stretching resources too thin. If you feel like you have more than 5, create them. Just keep in mind that each persona should provide actionable insights, making your marketing efforts more precise and effective. Larger companies or those in highly segmented markets might develop ten or more personas to capture the complexity of their audience effectively.

Each persona should include specific details that will influence how you tailor your marketing strategies, such as age, gender, education level, income, job title, and geographic location. Additionally, it's crucial to delve into psychographic factors like personality, values, opinions, attitudes, interests, and lifestyles. By understanding these elements, you can craft messages that resonate deeply and drive engagement.

CHAPTER 2 — Setting Up for Success

Template for creating your customer persona:

Basic Demographic Information
- Name: (Fictional name for persona)
- Age:
- Gender:
- Marital Status:
- Location: (Urban/Suburban/Rural, specific region or city)
- Education Level:
- Occupation:
- Income Level:

Psychographic Characteristics
- Personality Traits: (e.g., introverted, extroverted, pragmatic, idealistic)
- Values: (What core values motivate their decisions? E.g., sustainability, cost-efficiency, luxury)
- Interests: (Hobbies, leisure activities)
- Lifestyle: (Active, sedentary, family-oriented, travel-focused)
- Challenges and Pain Points: (What problems do they face that your product/service can solve?)
- Goals and Aspirations: (Both personal and professional)

Media Consumption
- Preferred Social Media Platforms: (Facebook, Instagram, LinkedIn, etc.)
- Favorite Websites: (For news, information, entertainment)
- Preferred Content Types: (Videos, articles, podcasts)
- Device Usage: (Smartphone, tablet, desktop, wearables)

Shopping Preferences and Behaviors
- Preferred Shopping Channels: (Online, in-store, both)
- Product Research Habits: (How do they research products? What factors influence their buying decisions?)
- Brand Loyalties: (Which brands do they love and why?)
- Purchase Drivers: (Price, quality, brand reputation, reviews)
- Frequency of Purchases: (Daily, weekly, monthly, occasionally)

Communication Preferences
- Preferred Contact Method: (Email, phone, text, in-person)
- Response to Promotions: (Coupons, free trials, demos, loyalty programs)
- Openness to Engagement: (How do they feel about interacting with brands?)

CHAPTER 2 — Setting Up for Success

Decision-Making Process
 - Key Influencers: (Who or what impacts their buying decisions? Family, friends, influencers, experts)
 - Role in Household Purchasing: (Primary decision-maker, influencer, or follower)
 - Decision Time Frame: (Impulse buyer or careful planner)

Professional Information: (For B2B Personas)
 - Industry:
 - Company Size:
 - Position:
 - Work Challenges:
 - Professional Goals:

Example Usage

When you have filled out this template, you will have a robust profile that helps you visualize your target customer, tailor your marketing strategies, create more relevant content, and ultimately, make more informed business decisions. For instance, if you know that your persona "John" is a tech-savvy young professional who values sustainability and spends a lot of time on social media platforms like LinkedIn and Twitter, you might focus your efforts on targeted advertising on these platforms with content that highlights the eco-friendly aspects of your products.

CHAPTER 2 Setting Up for Success

SEGMENTING YOUR AUDIENCE FOR TARGETED MARKETING

Once you have defined your customer personas, the next step is to segment your audience based on those personas and other relevant criteria. Audience segmentation involves dividing a broad customer base into smaller groups of individuals who share similar characteristics and thus are likely to respond similarly to your marketing strategies. Common bases for segmentation include:

Demographic Segmentation: Categorizing the audience by age, gender, income, occupation, etc. This type of segmentation helps tailor marketing messages according to the basic characteristics that may affect consumer needs and preferences.

- Example: A cosmetics company might target different product lines to women in different age groups, acknowledging that skin care needs vary by age.

Geographic Segmentation: Grouping customers by location, which can range from broad regions to specific cities or neighborhoods. Localized marketing campaigns can address climate, cultural, and regional differences.

- Example: A clothing retailer may promote winter gear in colder regions and lighter clothing options in warmer areas.

Psychographic Segmentation: Differentiating based on personal attributes like lifestyle, values, interests, and attitudes. This type of segmentation digs deeper into the consumer's psyche to better align marketing messages with their values and desires.

- Example: A travel agency creates distinct travel packages for adventure seekers and luxury travelers.

CHAPTER 2 — Setting Up for Success

Behavioral Segmentation: Classifying based on behaviors and patterns such as purchase history, brand loyalty, product usage, and feedback.

- Example: An online store might send special discount offers to first-time buyers while sending loyalty rewards to repeat customers.

Needs-Based Segmentation: Identify and group customers based on their specific needs and requirements.

- Example: A software company might segment its market into small businesses, mid-sized businesses, and large enterprises, offering tailored solutions to each group.

Value-Based Segmentation: This involves segmenting customers based on their economic value to the business, allowing you to focus more resources on high-value customers.

- Example: A premium service might be offered exclusively to the top-tier spending customers, enhancing their experience and retention.

Segmentation allows you to tailor your marketing efforts more precisely, which not only increases the effectiveness of your campaigns but also enhances customer satisfaction by providing more relevant content and offers. For instance, email marketing campaigns can be customized to address the specific needs and desires of different segments, thereby increasing the chances of engagement and conversion.

Effective segmentation leads to personalized marketing, which is crucial in today's market where consumers expect relevance and personal touch from brands. By understanding and implementing detailed customer personas and thoughtful segmentation, you can ensure that your marketing efforts reach the right audience with the right message at the right time, significantly boosting the efficiency and success of your marketing initiatives.

CHAPTER 2 Setting Up for Success

SETTING SMART GOALS FOR DIGITAL MARKETING

Understanding SMART Goals

SMART goals are specific, measurable, achievable, relevant, and time-bound objectives that guide your marketing efforts and ensure they lead to concrete outcomes. This approach helps focus your strategy and align your marketing activities with your overall business objectives.

Setting SMART goals in digital marketing is crucial for several reasons:

- Focus and direction: They provide clear guidance to your marketing team, helping everyone understand what needs to be accomplished.

- Resource allocation: They help in determining how to best use your resources to achieve maximum impact.

- Measurement and evaluation: They make it possible to track progress and measure success, which is essential for assessing the effectiveness of your campaigns and strategies.

- Motivation: They keep the team motivated and engaged, as clear, achievable goals give everyone something tangible to strive towards.

CHAPTER 2   **Setting Up for Success**

Components of SMART Goals

Specific: Your goal should be clear and specific to avoid misunderstandings. Specify what you want to accomplish, who needs to be involved, where it's going to happen, and any constraints or reasons.

e.g. Increase the monthly traffic of the new product blog by 30% through SEO and content updates.

Measurable: You should be able to measure your goal to track progress and know when it has been achieved. Decide on the metrics that will evidence your success.

e.g. Achieve 500 new sign-ups per month for our newsletter by launching a social media advertising campaign.

Achievable: Your goal also needs to be realistic and attainable to be successful. It should stretch your abilities but remain possible.

e.g. Boost sales by 15% in the next quarter by enhancing our e-commerce website's checkout process and implementing targeted email marketing campaigns.

Relevant: Ensure that your goal matters to your business and aligns with other objectives. It should be relevant to the direction you want your business to go.

e.g. Increase brand awareness by expanding our reach on social media by 25% within six months, aligning with our objective to enter new markets.

CHAPTER 2 Setting Up for Success

Time-bound: Every goal needs a target date, so that you have a deadline to focus on and something to work toward.

e.g. Generate an additional $100,000 in revenue from our online channels by the end of the financial year.

Implementing SMART Goals

Implementing SMART goals is a structured process that involves planning, executing, monitoring, and adjusting your strategies based on performance. This section details the steps you should take to effectively apply your SMART goals in digital marketing campaigns.

1. Detailed Planning

The first step in implementing your SMART goals is thorough planning. This involves:

Task Identification: Break down each goal into smaller, manageable tasks. Define what needs to be done, who will do it, and what resources will be required.

Timeline Creation: Establish deadlines for each task and overall milestones for the goal. Use a timeline that visualizes the entire project from start to finish.

Resource Allocation: Determine the resources needed to accomplish each task. This includes budgeting, manpower, tools, and other necessary materials.

Risk Assessment: Identify potential risks or obstacles that could hinder the achievement of your goals and plan contingency measures.

CHAPTER 2 — Setting Up for Success

2. Execution of Plans

With a solid plan in place, move to the execution phase:

Task Delegation: Assign tasks to team members based on their skills and capacities. Ensure everyone understands their responsibilities and the expectations.

Communication: Maintain open and consistent communication channels. Regular updates, team meetings, and progress reports help keep everyone aligned and focused.

Quality Control: Implement quality control measures to ensure that work meets the required standards. Regular checks and balances will help maintain the integrity of the campaign.

3. Monitoring Progress

Continuous monitoring is vital to ensure the plan is on track:

Performance Tracking: Use tools and software to track progress against the established metrics and KPIs. This can include analytics platforms, CRM software, and other digital marketing tools.

Adaptation and Flexibility: Be prepared to make adjustments as needed. Markets and technologies evolve, and your strategies may need tweaking to stay relevant and effective.

Feedback Loops: Create mechanisms for receiving feedback from all stakeholders, including team members, customers, and partners. Use this feedback to refine processes and improve performance.

CHAPTER 2: Setting Up for Success

4. Review and Adjustment

Finally, regularly review the entire process and make necessary adjustments:

Performance Review Meetings: Hold regular review meetings to assess what is working and what isn't. Discuss both successes and failures to understand the reasons behind them.

Learning and Development: Encourage a culture of learning from each campaign. Document lessons learned and integrate this knowledge into future planning.

Scaling and Optimization: For successful strategies, consider scaling up the efforts to maximize impact. For underperforming areas, apply the insights gained to optimize future campaigns.

5. Celebrating Successes

Recognizing and celebrating achievements is crucial for team morale and motivation:

Acknowledgment: Acknowledge individual and team contributions to achieving goals. Recognition can be as formal as award ceremonies or as simple as public commendation in meetings.

Rewards: Implement a rewards system to incentivize performance. This could range from bonuses and promotions to non-monetary rewards like extra vacation days or personal development opportunities.

CHAPTER 2 Setting Up for Success

BASICS OF A DIGITAL MARKETING STRATEGY

A digital marketing strategy is a plan that helps your business achieve specific digital goals through carefully selected online marketing channels such as paid, earned, and owned media. Whether you aim to increase brand awareness, boost sales, or retain customers, a well-crafted strategy is essential to guiding your actions and allocating resources efficiently.

Key Components of a Digital Marketing Strategy

Clear Objectives: Start with defining what you want to achieve. These should align with your broader business goals and be specific, measurable, achievable, relevant, and time-bound (SMART).

Audience Understanding: Know who you are targeting. Use data to create detailed customer personas (see Identifying your target audience section above) and segment your audience so that you can tailor your efforts to the right group of people.

Channel Selection: Decide which digital channels are best suited to reach your target audience effectively. Each channel, from social media to email, content marketing to SEO, has its strengths and should be chosen based on where your audience spends their time and what your goals are. This insight you'll also find through creating your customer personas.

CHAPTER 2 — Setting Up for Success

Content Planning: Developing a comprehensive content strategy is crucial for aligning your marketing efforts with your business goals. Start by determining the types of content that best engage your target audience, such as blog posts, videos, infographics, or social media updates, based on their preferences and the nature of the information you wish to convey. Assign content creation responsibilities clearly, whether to an in-house team, freelancers, or a mix, to ensure consistency in quality and voice. Plan your content publication schedule with a content calendar that specifies publication frequency and accounts for key industry events to maintain audience engagement and brand visibility.

Choose the right platforms for distributing your content, tailoring materials to fit the unique characteristics of each platform, like Instagram for visuals or LinkedIn for professional articles. Maintain flexibility in your strategy to adapt to feedback and changes in the market, regularly monitoring engagement and performance metrics to refine your approach. This dynamic and strategic planning ensures your content not only reaches but resonates with your audience, driving your marketing objectives forward effectively.

CHAPTER 2 Setting Up for Success

Budgeting: Effective budgeting in digital marketing is critical for allocating resources efficiently and ensuring that every dollar spent advances your business objectives. When planning your budget, it's important to account for all associated costs, including software tools, paid advertising, staff salaries, and content creation expenses.

For paid advertising, begin by defining clear objectives and setting measurable key performance indicators (KPIs) such as click-through rates or return on ad spend. Analyze historical data to identify which platforms and ad formats have previously performed well, guiding your budget allocation. Estimate costs based on average industry rates for cost-per-click (CPC) or cost-per-impression (CPM).

For example, if aiming for 1000 clicks per month at a CPC of $1, set aside $1000 for that campaign. Distribute your total advertising budget across platforms based on their ability to meet your strategic goals, allocating more to those with proven effectiveness. Continuously monitor campaign performance and adjust your budget allocation to optimize returns. Regular ROI analysis helps in refining your strategy, ensuring you maximize the impact and efficiency of your advertising spend. This comprehensive approach not only manages expenditures wisely but also enhances the overall success of your digital marketing efforts.

CHAPTER 2 — Setting Up for Success

Integration: Integrating your digital marketing strategy with your overall marketing plan is essential for creating a seamless and cohesive customer experience that effectively reinforces your brand message across all channels. This integration requires aligning digital goals with the broader objectives of your company's marketing strategy, ensuring that every digital effort enhances your overall business goals. Effective integration involves constant collaboration between digital and traditional marketing teams to synchronize messages and unify promotional activities, ensuring consistency whether a customer interacts with your brand online or offline.

Employing a cross-channel approach, such as promoting social media campaigns in print ads and using insights gathered from online interactions to personalize offline marketing, can amplify your efforts and provide a comprehensive understanding of customer behaviors. Technology plays a crucial role here, with marketing automation tools aiding in managing customer interactions across channels, maintaining consistent messaging, and adapting strategies based on real-time data.

By maintaining uniformity in branding, tone, and messaging across all marketing materials, your strategy not only becomes more effective but also helps solidify your brand identity in the marketplace, leading to enhanced customer engagement and increased conversion rates.

CHAPTER 2 — Setting Up for Success

Analytics and Measurement: To maximize the effectiveness and continual improvement of your digital marketing strategies, establishing a comprehensive system for analytics and measurement is essential. By leveraging sophisticated analytics tools, you can track crucial metrics such as website traffic, conversion rates, user engagement, and overall return on investment (ROI). These tools help you to understand the impact of your marketing efforts and identify which aspects are performing well versus those that might need adjustments. It's important to align the metrics you track with your specific marketing objectives—focusing on page views and social media interactions for brand awareness objectives, or conversion rates for sales-oriented goals.

Platforms such as Google Analytics, social media analytics, and CRM systems provide detailed insights into customer behavior and interaction with your campaigns. Regular analysis of these data points allows you to spot trends and make informed decisions about where to allocate resources, how to tweak your campaigns, and when to pivot your strategies. Integrating this data with A/B testing further refines your approach by empirically determining which variations of your marketing materials perform best, enabling targeted adjustments.

This cycle of measuring, analyzing, and refining is crucial for adapting to changes in consumer behavior and the digital market, ensuring your marketing efforts are both effective and efficient over time.

CHAPTER 2 — Setting Up for Success

MOST POPULAR FRAMEWORKS FOR MARKETING EXPLAINED

1. The 7 Ps of Marketing

The 7 Ps of Marketing framework enhances the classic 4 Ps model by adding three additional elements—People, Process, and Physical evidence. This expansion provides a more holistic view of what a marketing mix can and should entail, especially in a service-centric or customer-focused business environment. Understanding and implementing each of the 7 Ps can greatly enhance the effectiveness of your marketing strategies by addressing all aspects of the customer experience.

1. Product

   - Definition: The goods or services that your business offers to meet the needs and wants of your target market.

   - Considerations: Quality, design, features, branding, and product variety are all crucial. A robust product strategy must also consider the product lifecycle and how market needs might evolve.

2. Price

   - Definition: What the customer pays to obtain the product or service.

   - Considerations: Pricing strategies can include cost-based pricing, value-based pricing, and competitive pricing. Factors like discounts, financing, and leasing options also play a role in how accessible your product is to different segments of the market.

CHAPTER 2 — Setting Up for Success

3. Place
   - Definition: Where and how your products or services are available to consumers.

   - Considerations: This can involve selecting appropriate distribution channels, managing supply chains, and considering the geographic location of your target markets. The goal is to make it as easy as possible for customers to find and purchase your offerings.

4. Promotion
   - Definition: The activities that make your target audience aware of your products or services and persuade them to make a purchase.

   - Considerations: This includes advertising, sales promotions, public relations, direct marketing, and digital marketing efforts. Each promotional activity should be aligned with the overall brand message and marketing goals.

5. People
   - Definition: Everyone involved in both the production and delivery of the product or service, from employees to customers.

   - Considerations: Staff training, customer service policies, and the overall culture of the organization are essential. The people representing your brand can significantly impact the customer's experience and perception of your value.

CHAPTER 2 Setting Up for Success

6. Process
- Definition: The procedures, mechanisms, and flow of activities by which services are consumed.

- Considerations: This includes the customer service process, the sales process, and the delivery process. Having efficient and customer-friendly processes is crucial for ensuring customer satisfaction and can differentiate a company in competitive markets.

7. Physical Evidence
- Definition: The environment in which the service is delivered and where the company and customer interact, as well as any tangible components that facilitate performance or communication of the service.

- Considerations: This can be the layout of a retail store, the design of a website, or even the packaging of a product. Physical evidence helps to make the service experience tangible and assures customers of the quality of service they are receiving.

By carefully analyzing and optimizing each of the 7 Ps, you can create a more compelling and competitive marketing mix that addresses all facets of the customer journey. This framework not only helps in aligning marketing strategies more closely with the broader operational and strategic goals of an organization but also enhances the ability to deliver superior value to customers.

CHAPTER 2 Setting Up for Success

2. AIDA Model

The AIDA model is a classic marketing framework that outlines the cognitive stages a customer goes through before making a purchase decision. It stands for Attention, Interest, Desire, and Action, representing the sequential steps that marketing efforts should facilitate to effectively guide a potential customer toward purchasing a product or service.

1. Attention (Awareness)

- Objective: Capture the potential customer's attention.

- Strategies: Employ impactful advertising, vibrant social media campaigns, eye-catching content, and public relations efforts. The key is to stand out from the competition and make the audience notice your brand or product. For digital campaigns, this might involve using SEO tactics to appear in search results or visually appealing ads in various media formats.

- Importance: This is the crucial first step where you make a first impression. Without gaining attention, no further steps in the sales process can occur.

2. Interest

- Objective: Once you have their attention, the next step is to cultivate their interest by focusing on how your products or services solve their problems or improve their situation.

- Strategies: Provide informative and engaging content that is relevant to the audience, such as blogs, videos, podcasts, or newsletters that explain the benefits and features of your offerings. This is about making the potential customer see the unique value proposition of your products.

CHAPTER 2 Setting Up for Success

   - Importance: Interest is deepened by offering knowledge and solutions that are aligned with what the customer truly cares about, thus setting the stage for a deeper engagement.

3. Desire
   - Objective: Convert their interest into a desire for your product or service. This is where you make them feel that they want what you're offering.

   - Strategies: Use emotional appeal and testimonials to enhance the attractiveness of your offer. Detailed case studies, user reviews, and vivid product descriptions help the customer visualize the benefits they'll gain, intensifying their emotional connection and desire.

   - Importance: Desire bridges the gap between liking something in principle and wanting to incorporate it into one's life. It involves creating a personal connection and a sense of need.

4. Action
   - Objective: Encourage the potential customer to take the next step or make a purchase.

   - Strategies: This final step should include a clear, compelling call to action (CTA), special promotions, and incentives like discounts or limited-time offers. Ensure the purchasing process is as easy and frictionless as possible to maximize conversion rates.

   - Importance: This is the culmination of the marketing efforts, where interest and desire convert into actual sales. The action stage isn't just about making a sale; it's also about creating a seamless experience that can lead to further post-purchase engagement, such as repeat business and referrals.

CHAPTER 2 Setting Up for Success

Implementing the AIDA Model

Implementing the AIDA model effectively requires a well-coordinated marketing strategy that moves seamlessly from one stage to the next, maintaining the momentum gained from the first interaction. Each stage should be carefully planned and executed with targeted campaigns designed to push the customer closer to the purchase decision. Monitoring the effectiveness of strategies at each stage through metrics such as engagement rates, conversion rates, and sales figures is essential to understand the impact and to refine tactics continually.

This model serves as a powerful guide for creating marketing messages that resonate and motivate, ensuring that your marketing communications effectively lead potential customers through each stage of the buying process.

3. Customer Journey Mapping

Customer Journey Mapping is a strategic approach to understanding the steps your customers take as they engage with your product or service. This tool visualizes the customer's experience from initial awareness all the way through to purchase and beyond, capturing the key interactions and emotional experiences at each touchpoint. It helps businesses gain insights into common customer pain points, desires, and motivations, enabling them to tailor marketing and operational strategies more effectively.

1. Customer Personas:

Start by identifying your customer personas, which are detailed descriptions of your ideal customers. These personas are foundational for mapping as they represent different user needs and behaviors.

CHAPTER 2: Setting Up for Success

2. Phases of the Journey:
Break down the journey into distinct phases that the customer experiences. Common phases include Awareness, Consideration, Decision, Purchase, and Post-Purchase.

i. Awareness
   - Description: This is the initial stage where potential customers first become aware of your brand or product. They might not have a need yet, but your marketing efforts put you on their radar.
   - Key Activities: Utilize broad-reaching advertising, content marketing, social media presence, PR events, and SEO strategies.
   - Goal: To make potential customers aware of your brand as a potential solution to their future needs.

ii. Consideration
   - Description: At this stage, customers recognize that they have a need or a problem and consider various products or services to solve it. They are evaluating their options.
   - Key Activities: Provide detailed and informative content such as comparison guides, product demos, customer testimonials, and educational webinars.
   - Goal: To position your brand as a top contender for the customer's needs by highlighting unique selling propositions and benefits.

CHAPTER 2 — Setting Up for Success

iii. Decision
   - Description: Here, customers are close to making a purchase decision. They compare different offers, look into the specifics, and might seek opinions from others.
   - Key Activities: Offer promotions, free trials, or consultations; provide accessible customer service and detailed FAQs; showcase positive reviews and case studies.
   - Goal: To convince customers that your product or service is the best choice among competitors.

iv. Purchase
   - Description: The actual transaction takes place in this phase. Customers purchase the product or subscribe to the service.
   - Key Activities: Ensure a smooth checkout process, offer various payment options, and provide clear instructions and support for any issues that might arise.
   - Goal: To create a seamless and satisfactory purchasing experience that leaves a positive impression, encouraging future interaction.

v. Post-Purchase
   - Description: After making a purchase, customers evaluate their satisfaction with the product and the process. This stage is critical for retaining customers and encouraging repeat purchases.
   - Key Activities: Follow up with customers through thank-you emails, customer satisfaction surveys, and offers of additional support or products. Implement loyalty programs and request feedback.
   - Goal: To maintain customer satisfaction and loyalty, transforming new customers into repeat buyers and advocates for the brand.

CHAPTER 2 — Setting Up for Success

vi. Loyalty and Advocacy (optional extension)

- Description: In this extended phase, satisfied customers become loyal to the brand and are likely to make repeat purchases. They may also advocate for the brand through word-of-mouth, testimonials, or reviews.

- Key Activities: Engage with loyal customers through exclusive offers, insider information, and community-building activities. Encourage sharing of their positive experiences.

- Goal: To strengthen relationships with existing customers and expand reach through advocacy and referrals.

3. Touchpoints:

Identify all the points at which customers interact with your brand, whether online or offline. These can include visiting your website, receiving an email, talking to customer service, or seeing an ad.

e.g. John's Journey

Meet John, a 30-year-old software developer with a passion for photography. He's recently been on the lookout for a new camera to take his hobby to the next level. Let's follow John's journey through various touchpoints with an eCommerce store specializing in photography equipment.

<u>Awareness:</u>
John's journey begins one evening as he browses through his favorite photography blog. An eye-catching banner ad for a new high-end camera appears on the sidebar—placed by the eCommerce store. Curious, John clicks on the ad, which takes him to the store's landing page dedicated to the latest camera models.

CHAPTER 2 — Setting Up for Success

Interest:
Intrigued by the array of camera options, John signs up for the store's newsletter to receive updates on new arrivals, tips on photography, and special promotions. A few days later, he receives a welcome email with a 10% discount on his first purchase. The email also includes links to top-selling products and a beginner's guide to choosing cameras, which keeps him engaged and wanting to learn more.

Consideration:
John spends the next few weeks visiting the eCommerce site multiple times. He reads through product descriptions, watches video reviews embedded on the product pages, and browses customer testimonials. The site's comparison tool allows him to view different cameras side-by-side, helping him narrow down his choices based on features and prices.

Intent:
Having decided on a specific model, John uses the live chat feature on the website to ask some last-minute questions about the camera. The customer service representative provides helpful information and mentions an ongoing sale that includes free accessories with the camera. Feeling confident, John adds the camera to his cart.

Purchase:
John proceeds to checkout, where he uses the discount code from his welcome email. The checkout process is smooth and straightforward. He chooses his preferred payment method and completes the transaction. Shortly after, he receives a confirmation email detailing his purchase and expected delivery date.

CHAPTER 2 — Setting Up for Success

Post-Purchase:
John receives regular updates via email on his order status. Upon receiving his camera, he also gets an email asking for feedback on his shopping experience and the product. Pleased with the purchase, John leaves a positive review and signs up for a membership program that offers points for each dollar spent.

Loyalty:
Over the next several months, John receives personalized emails based on his interests, including special offers on camera lenses and photography workshops. The store also invites him to join their exclusive online community of photography enthusiasts.

Advocacy:
Impressed with the quality of service and products, John becomes a brand advocate. He refers several friends to the store, shares his positive experiences on social media, and continues to engage with the store's content. For his engagement and referrals, the store rewards him with exclusive offers, enhancing his loyalty and satisfaction.

Conclusion:
John's journey from awareness to advocacy highlights the critical touchpoints that an eCommerce business must manage to provide a seamless, engaging customer experience. Each stage of the journey presents an opportunity to solidify the relationship, turning a casual browser into a loyal customer and advocate.

CHAPTER 2 — Setting Up for Success

4. Customer Emotions:

Chart the emotions and attitudes customers have at each touchpoint. Understanding emotional highs and lows is crucial for optimizing the customer experience.

In order to understand these, you can:
- send out surveys and feedback forms
- do customer interviews or focus groups (especially feasible in service)
- do sentiment analysis (meaning analyzing the customer reviews, social media comments, and other customer communications)
- analyze behavioral data (Observing how customers behave can provide indirect clues about their emotional states. For example, high abandonment rates at a particular stage in an online process might indicate frustration or confusion).

5. Channels:

Document the channels through which interactions occur at each touchpoint, such as social media, mobile apps, or in-store visits.

Awareness Stage
- Social Media Platforms: Facebook, Instagram, Twitter, LinkedIn, Pinterest
- Search Engines: Google, Bing (via SEO and PPC campaigns)
- Display Ads: Banner ads on websites, retargeting ads
- Video Platforms: YouTube, Vimeo (for video ads and informational content)
- Influencer Partnerships: Collaborations on social media or blogs
- Podcasts: Advertising or guest appearances on relevant podcasts

CHAPTER 2 — Setting Up for Success

Interest Stage
- Email Newsletters: Regular updates and educational content sent to subscribers
- Blogs and Articles: Content hosted on your own site or on third-party publications
- Webinars and Live Streams: Educational sessions hosted on platforms like Zoom, Facebook Live
- Social Media: Continued engagement through posts, stories, and community interactions

Consideration Stage
- Product Review Sites: Third-party sites where users review products
- Comparison Shopping Engines: Platforms like Google Shopping where users compare product features and prices
- FAQ Sections and Knowledge Bases: Information hubs on your website
- Customer Service Channels: Live chat, email support, or help desks

Intent Stage
- Shopping Cart on Website or Mobile App: Where customers add products before purchasing
- Email: Follow-up messages for cart abandonment or to answer specific queries
- Mobile Apps: Push notifications for offers or reminders

Purchase Stage
- E-commerce Website: Secure checkout pages
- Mobile Apps: In-app purchasing capabilities
- Payment Gateways: PayPal, Apple Pay, credit/debit card processing interfaces

CHAPTER 2 Setting Up for Success

Post-Purchase Stage
- Email: Order confirmation, shipping updates, and feedback requests
- SMS: Text updates for order processing and delivery
- Customer Portals: Account pages where customers can track their order history

Loyalty Stage
- Loyalty Program Platforms: Apps or websites where customers can check their rewards points and redeem offers
- Email and Social Media: Special offers and exclusive content for returning customers
- Events and Community Engagements: Online or physical events for loyal customers

Advocacy Stage
- Social Media: Platforms where satisfied customers can share their experiences and tag the brand
- Review Platforms: Sites like Yelp, Trustpilot, or industry-specific review sites
- Referral Programs: Platforms or tools that facilitate and reward customers for referring friends

6. Pain Points and Opportunities:

Identify any difficulties customers face along their journey, as well as opportunities where your brand can enhance the customer experience. The most common way of doing this is through customer feedback.

CHAPTER 2 — Setting Up for Success

Benefits of Customer Journey Mapping

- Enhanced Customer Understanding: Provides deep insights into customer needs and behaviors.

- Improved Customer Experience: Helps pinpoint problem areas where customers might drop off or feel dissatisfied.

- Increased Cross-Functional Collaboration: Encourages a unified approach to customer experience across the organization.

- Greater Strategic Alignment: Aligns business processes and customer touchpoints with the overall customer experience goals.

STP Model (Segmentation, Targeting, Positioning)

The STP Model is a powerful framework used in marketing to sharpen the effectiveness of marketing campaigns. It breaks down the process into three key steps: Segmentation, Targeting, and Positioning. This approach helps businesses to be more focused and efficient in reaching their audience and aligning their products or services with market needs. Here's a detailed look at each step:

i. Segmentation

- Definition: Segmentation involves dividing a broad consumer or business market into sub-groups of consumers (known as segments) based on some type of shared characteristics. This can include demographic, psychographic, geographic, or behavioral attributes.

- Purpose: The goal of market segmentation is to identify high-yield segments — that is, those segments that are likely to be the most profitable or that have growth potential — so that these can be selected for special attention (i.e., targeted).

CHAPTER 2 — Setting Up for Success

- Methods:
  - Demographic Segmentation: Splitting the market based on variables such as age, gender, family size, income, occupation, education, and more.

  - Geographic Segmentation: Organizing the market based on geography such as region, country, state, or even neighborhood.

  - Psychographic Segmentation: Dividing the market based on social class, lifestyle, or personality characteristics.

  - Behavioral Segmentation: Segmenting the market based on consumer knowledge, attitudes, uses, or responses to a product.

ii. Targeting

- Definition: After the market has been segmented into its subsets, the marketer will select a segment or series of segments and 'target' them. Targeting is the process of evaluating each segment's attractiveness and selecting one or more segments to enter.

- Purpose: To focus marketing dollars and brand messages on a specific market that is more likely to buy than other segments. This efficiency helps the company to gain a competitive advantage in the segment.

- Approaches:
  - Undifferentiated Targeting: Targeting the whole market with one offer, focusing on what is common in the needs of consumers rather than on what is different.

  - Differentiated Targeting: Targeting several market segments with a different offering for each.

CHAPTER 2 — Setting Up for Success

   - Concentrated Targeting: Targeting a large share of a small market segment. This strategy is often used by smaller firms.

   - Micro or Local Marketing: Tailoring products and marketing programs to the needs and wants of local customer groups — cities, neighborhoods, specific stores.

iii. Positioning
- Definition: The final stage, positioning, involves the process of defining the marketing mix variables so that target customers have a clear, distinctive, desirable understanding of what the product does or represents in comparison with competing products.

- Purpose: Positioning is crucial as it helps consumers perceive and comprehend the distinct attributes of your product compared to competing products.

- Strategies:
  - Value Positioning: Positioning based on the product or service's value - the best price or quality.

  - Product Attributes: Positioning based on specific attributes or benefits of the product.

  - Use or Application: Positioning according to product use or application.

  - Competitor-Based: Positioning directly against a competitor's offering.

  - Perceptual Mapping: Using perceptual maps to visualize the positioning of competing products.

CHAPTER 2 | Setting Up for Success

Implementing the STP Model

Applying the STP model involves continuous research and monitoring to adjust strategies based on market dynamics and consumer behavior. It requires a deep understanding of the market and the ability to adapt marketing strategies to meet the challenges of targeting and positioning effectively. By effectively segmenting the market, accurately targeting segments, and positioning products distinctly, companies can achieve a stronger market presence, greater sales, and better overall effectiveness of their marketing strategy.

4 Cs Marketing Model

The 4 Cs Marketing Model offers a shift from the traditional 4 Ps (Product, Price, Place, Promotion) by focusing more intensely on the needs of the customer rather than the perspective of the marketer. Developed by Robert F. Lauterborn, this model emphasizes the importance of customer interests in the marketing process. The 4 Cs are Customer needs and wants, Cost to satisfy, Convenience to buy, and Communication. Here's a detailed look at each component:

i. Customer Needs and Wants

- Definition: This component shifts the focus from the product itself to the needs and wants of the customer. It's about understanding what solutions customers are actually looking for, which may not necessarily align with the product as originally designed.

- Purpose: To tailor products and services to better meet the real and evolving needs of target customers.

- Application: Conducting extensive market research and ongoing dialogue with customers to continuously adapt and innovate products or services based on customer feedback and changing demands.

CHAPTER 2 | Setting Up for Success

ii. Cost to Satisfy
- Definition: This replaces the traditional "Price" element and looks at the total cost to the customer to satisfy their need. This includes not only the purchase price but also additional costs associated with acquiring, using, and maintaining the product or service.

- Purpose: To understand and minimize the total cost for customers, making the product not only affordable but also providing greater value for money.

- Application: Analyzing all cost elements customers face and finding ways to reduce them—whether through more efficient product design, lower pricing strategies, bundled offers, or improved product longevity.

iii. Convenience to Buy
- Definition: This component modernizes the idea of 'Place'. Convenience to buy focuses on how easy it is for the customer to make the purchase, reflecting the modern consumer's preference for a hassle-free shopping experience.

- Purpose: To make purchasing as convenient as possible, thereby increasing the likelihood of sales.

- Application: Ensuring the product is available where and when customers need it, utilizing multiple channels for distribution, and simplifying the buying process through technological enhancements like mobile apps, online shopping, and efficient delivery systems.

CHAPTER 2: Setting Up for Success

iv. Communication

- Definition: Replacing 'Promotion', this element highlights the importance of two-way communication rather than one-way selling messages. It emphasizes engaging with customers through dialogues that inform, educate, and resonate emotionally.

- Purpose: To build stronger relationships with customers by listening to their needs and feedback, and communicating effectively about how products and services can fulfill their expectations.

- Application: Utilizing social media, customer service platforms, feedback loops, content marketing, and personalized communications to create meaningful interactions and a community around the brand.

Implementing the 4 Cs Marketing Model

Adopting the 4 Cs model involves a paradigm shift in how a business approaches its market strategy. It requires deep customer insights gathered through robust data analytics and direct customer interactions. Companies must be agile, ready to innovate in response to customer feedback, and willing to adopt new technologies and methods for effective communication and distribution.

Ultimately, the 4 Cs model aims to create a more customer-centric approach in marketing efforts, ensuring that strategies are not only aligned with the company's objectives but also resonate deeply with the needs and preferences of the market. This approach can lead to higher customer satisfaction, enhanced brand loyalty, and a stronger competitive edge in the marketplace.

CHAPTER 2 — Setting Up for Success

Content Marketing Matrix

The Content Marketing Matrix is a valuable tool for marketers to effectively tailor content strategies to different stages of the buying cycle. It helps in visualizing the impact of various types of content on customer engagement and decision-making, providing a structured approach to content creation and distribution. By aligning content with the customer's journey, marketers can more effectively influence and support the customer's path to purchase.

Overview of the Content Marketing Matrix

The matrix categorizes content based on its purpose and the level of engagement it seeks to elicit from the audience. The two main axes are:

- Y-Axis (Emotional to Rational): This axis represents the emotional appeal of the content to more rational, informative content. Emotional content aims to create a connection and resonate on a personal level, while rational content seeks to inform and educate.

- X-Axis (Entertain to Inspire): This axis ranges from content designed purely to entertain and capture attention to content that aims to inspire action or change in behavior.

CHAPTER 2 — Setting Up for Success

Four Quadrants of the Content Marketing Matrix

1. Entertain & Inform (Top Left Quadrant)
- Purpose: To engage customers at the initial stages of the buying cycle where awareness and interest are the focus.
- Content Types: Viral videos, interactive infographics, quizzes, and games.
- Goals: To capture attention and engage users in a light, enjoyable manner.

2. Inform & Educate (Top Right Quadrant)
- Purpose: To provide value through educational content that informs customers about specific topics, helping them make informed decisions.
- Content Types: How-to guides, tutorials, webinars, white papers, and industry reports.
- Goals: To build trust and establish brand authority by offering depth and detail.

3. Entertain & Inspire (Bottom Left Quadrant)
- Purpose: To create inspirational content that encourages brand interaction through emotional engagement.
- Content Types: Inspirational stories, motivational videos, and impactful case studies.
- Goals: To connect emotionally and motivate the audience towards a specific attitude or action.

4. Inspire & Persuade (Bottom Right Quadrant)
- Purpose: To drive conversion by combining rational arguments with inspirational elements that persuade customers to take action.
- Content Types: Customer testimonials, product reviews, live demos, and persuasive articles.
- Goals: To influence decision-making and encourage the audience to commit to a purchase.

CHAPTER 2 — Setting Up for Success

Implementing the Content Marketing Matrix

- Identify Audience Needs: Understand what your audience seeks at different stages of their journey. This helps in determining whether they need information, entertainment, inspiration, or persuasion.

- Create a Content Plan: Develop a content plan that incorporates a variety of content types across the matrix. Ensure each piece serves a strategic purpose in moving customers along the buying cycle.

- Measure and Optimize: Continuously measure the effectiveness of different content types and refine your strategy based on analytics. Look at engagement metrics, conversion rates, and customer feedback to assess performance.

- Align with Marketing Goals: Ensure that all content is aligned with broader marketing goals and contributes to the overall strategy. This coherence maximizes the impact of your content on customer engagement and business objectives.

CHAPTER 2 Setting Up for Success

RACE Framework

The RACE Framework is a strategic model designed to help marketers plan and manage their digital marketing activities more effectively. Developed by Smart Insights, RACE stands for Reach, Act, Convert, and Engage, each representing a crucial stage in the customer journey. This framework provides a structured approach to capturing and interacting with customers from their initial contact through to a long-term relationship.

1. Reach

<u>Objective:</u> The primary goal during the Reach phase is to build awareness of your brand, products, or services among your target audience. This stage focuses on using various marketing tactics to attract your audience to your platforms.

<u>Activities:</u>
- SEO (Search Engine Optimization): Optimizing website content to ensure high visibility in search engine results for relevant keywords.

- PPC (Pay Per Click) Advertising: Running paid campaigns on search engines and social media to drive traffic.

- Social Media Marketing: Utilizing platforms like Facebook, Instagram, and Twitter to spread awareness and reach potential customers.

- Content Marketing: Publishing informative and engaging content that draws audiences to your blogs, videos, and other media forms.

<u>Metrics:</u> Key metrics include impressions, reach, traffic volumes, and new visitors.

CHAPTER 2 Setting Up for Success

2. Act

<u>Objective:</u> This stage is about persuading your audience to take the next step — an interaction that goes beyond just browsing. It's about encouraging actions that don't necessarily result in a sale but prepare the ground for one.

<u>Activities:</u>
- Lead Generation Forms: Encouraging visitors to fill out contact forms or subscribe to newsletters.
- Content Engagement: Engaging users with interactive content, polls, or ebooks that require active participation.
- Social Media Interaction: Promoting shares, comments, and likes to build community interactions.

<u>Metrics:</u> Metrics here include time on site, page views per visit, social interaction rates, and lead conversion rates.

3. Convert

<u>Objective:</u> The Convert phase aims to transform interactions into transactions. This is where direct selling occurs, and marketing efforts are focused on making the sale.

<u>Activities:</u>
- E-commerce Funnels: Streamlining the online purchasing process to minimize abandonment and maximize conversion.
- Retargeting Campaigns: Using retargeting to bring back visitors who didn't convert on their first visit.
- Promotions and Offers: Implementing time-limited offers or exclusive deals to incentivize immediate purchases.

<u>Metrics:</u> Conversion rates, sales, average order value, and cost per conversion are critical metrics in this phase.

CHAPTER 2: Setting Up for Success

4. Engage

Objective: After converting customers, the Engage phase focuses on developing long-term relationships to foster repeat sales, loyalty, and advocacy.

Activities:
- Email Marketing: Sending targeted messages to existing customers to encourage repeat purchases and keep your brand top-of-mind.

- Loyalty Programs: Implementing programs that reward repeat customers with discounts, offers, or other benefits.

- Customer Feedback: Collecting and acting on customer feedback to improve the product or service.

Metrics: Repeat purchase rate, customer lifetime value, net promoter score, and retention rate are important here.

Implementing the RACE Framework

To implement the RACE Framework effectively, businesses should integrate these activities into their digital marketing strategies, ensuring each stage is tailored to move the customer along the journey. It requires continuous monitoring and optimization based on performance analytics to understand what is working and what needs adjustment.

By following the RACE framework, marketers can ensure a holistic approach to managing customer interactions across the digital spectrum, enhancing every touchpoint in the customer journey, and ultimately driving business success.

CHAPTER 2 — Setting Up for Success

Marketing Sales Funnel

The Marketing Sales Funnel is a model used to outline the process of turning leads into customers. By visualizing the customer journey as a funnel, marketers can better understand how to effectively guide potential customers through each stage, from initial awareness to the final purchase decision. This funnel framework not only helps in strategizing various marketing activities but also in optimizing conversions and improving overall sales effectiveness.

Stages of the Marketing Sales Funnel
Awareness
- Objective: The top of the funnel is all about generating awareness of your brand, product, or service. At this stage, potential customers are just beginning to learn about what you offer.
- Activities: Use broad-reaching marketing tactics like SEO, PPC, social media advertising, content marketing, and public relations to attract a wide audience.
- Goal: To inform the target audience about your brand and make a memorable first impression.

Interest
- Objective: Once you have their attention, the goal is to cultivate their interest by providing more information about how your products or services can solve their problems or improve their situation.
- Activities: Engage users through targeted content like newsletters, blogs, e-books, and more detailed social media posts. This content should help build a relationship by educating and offering value.
- Goal: To engage potential customers and make them interested in learning more about your offerings.

CHAPTER 2 — Setting Up for Success

Consideration
- Objective: At this mid-funnel stage, potential customers are considering whether or not to purchase your product or engage with your service. They compare you against competitors and evaluate what you offer.
- Activities: Utilize targeted marketing strategies such as email marketing, retargeting ads, and personalized content to nurture leads. Product demos, customer testimonials, and case studies are effective here.
- Goal: To nurture the relationship and solidify your brand as the best choice.

Intent
- Objective: Leads at this stage show a strong inclination towards purchasing but might need a final nudge to complete the action.
- Activities: This is where you can use promotions, limited-time offers, or free trials to encourage a decision. Sales teams may also engage directly with leads to address any last-minute concerns.
- Goal: To motivate leads to make a decision and move forward to the purchase stage.

Conversion
- Objective: The bottom of the funnel is where the actual purchase happens.
- Activities: Ensure that the purchasing process is as smooth as possible with a straightforward checkout process, multiple payment options, and excellent customer support.
- Goal: To convert interested leads into customers

CHAPTER 2 — Setting Up for Success

Loyalty
- Objective: After a purchase, the focus shifts to turning new customers into repeat buyers and loyal advocates of your brand.
- Activities: Implement post-purchase follow-ups, loyalty programs, and request feedback to enhance customer satisfaction. Continue engaging with them through personalized communications and offers.
- Goal: To maintain a positive relationship, encourage loyalty, and increase the likelihood of repeat purchases.

Advocacy
- Objective: Satisfied customers are encouraged to share their positive experiences with others, expanding your reach organically.
- Activities: Encourage reviews, testimonials, and referrals. Engage advocates through community-building activities and recognition.
- Goal: To transform satisfied customers into active promoters of your brand.

Implementing the Marketing Sales Funnel

To effectively utilize the Marketing Sales Funnel, each stage must be carefully planned with strategic activities designed to move the customer to the next phase. Continuous monitoring and analysis of each stage are crucial to identify bottlenecks or drop-off points and to optimize strategies accordingly. By understanding and enhancing each phase of the funnel, marketers can significantly improve the efficiency of their sales process, boost conversions, and ultimately drive more revenue.

CHAPTER 2 — Setting Up for Success

TOFU-MOFU-BOFU

The TOFU, MOFU, BOFU framework is indeed another way to describe the marketing funnel, focusing more explicitly on the content strategy at each stage of the customer journey. TOFU (Top of Funnel), MOFU (Middle of Funnel), and BOFU (Bottom of Funnel) break down the traditional funnel into distinct phases that are closely aligned with the customer's decision-making process. This framework can provide more detailed guidance on how to approach content creation and marketing tactics tailored to each stage. Here's a breakdown of each:

TOFU (Top of Funnel)

- Objective: Raise awareness and attract new leads.

- Content Types: Blogs, social media posts, infographics, informational videos, and eBooks that are designed to educate, inform, and draw in a broad audience. The key is to focus on general interest content that can attract the maximum number of potential leads.

- Activities: SEO to enhance visibility, social media engagement to widen reach, and educational content to spark interest and attract website traffic.

MOFU (Middle of Funnel)

- Objective: Engage and nurture the leads you've gathered who have shown some interest in your brand.

- Content Types: More detailed content such as webinars, case studies, deep-dive articles, and email newsletters that begin to introduce your products or services in a subtle way. The focus is on building trust and establishing your brand as a thought leader in your industry.

- Activities: Lead nurturing programs such as targeted email marketing, retargeting campaigns, and personalized content to build a deeper relationship with prospects.

CHAPTER 2 Setting Up for Success

BOFU (Bottom of Funnel)
- Objective: Convert leads into customers.

- Content Types: Product demos, free trials, customer testimonials, and detailed product information that help to close the sale. At this stage, content should be highly targeted and conversion-focused, addressing specific barriers to purchase and emphasizing the value proposition.

- Activities: Direct sales outreach, special discount offers, consultation calls, and strong calls-to-action (CTAs) that encourage a purchase decision.

Applying the TOFU, MOFU, BOFU Framework
- Customization: Tailor content and marketing tactics to the mindset and needs of prospects at each stage. This means understanding what information they need next to move them further along in their decision-making process.

- Alignment: Ensure that each stage feeds into the next. Prospects should be guided smoothly from one stage to the next with clear pathways and calls to action, such as subscribing, signing up, or contacting sales.

- Measurement and Optimization: Just like any marketing strategy, it's vital to measure the effectiveness of your tactics at each stage. Use analytics to track progress and optimize based on what's working or areas where prospects might be dropping off.

While similar to the traditional marketing funnel, the TOFU, MOFU, BOFU framework emphasizes the progression of content strategy in tandem with the buyer's journey, making it a valuable tool for marketers who are specifically focused on content-driven engagement strategies. This model can be particularly useful in a content-rich environment where educating and nurturing leads through information and trust-building is key to conversion.

CHAPTER 3
Developing a Content Strategy

IMPORTANCE OF CONTENT MARKETING

Content marketing is a strategic approach focused on creating and distributing valuable, relevant, and consistent content to attract and retain a clearly-defined audience — ultimately, to drive profitable customer action. This marketing discipline is essential for several compelling reasons:

1. Building Trust and Credibility

Foundation of Trust: Regularly providing your customers with helpful and informative content establishes your brand as a trustworthy and credible source in your industry. This trust is crucial for building long-term relationships with your audience.

Expertise Demonstration: High-quality content that addresses customer questions and concerns showcases your expertise and leadership in your field, further cementing trust.

2. Supporting the Buyer's Journey

Awareness and Education: Content marketing plays a vital role at every stage of the buyer's journey. Initially, it helps to educate potential customers about their needs and introduces solutions, subtly guiding them from awareness to consideration.

Decision Making: As potential customers move closer to a purchase decision, detailed content such as case studies, testimonials, and product comparisons can provide the essential information needed to convert them from interested prospects into paying customers.

CHAPTER 3: Developing a Content Strategy

3. Enhancing SEO Efforts

<u>Search Engine Visibility:</u> Content is a key element in search engine optimization. Search engines favor fresh, relevant content, and publishing articles, blogs, and other forms of content consistently can boost your site's visibility and ranking.

<u>Keyword Integration:</u> Strategic use of keywords in your content can attract more traffic to your pages, making it easier for potential customers to find you online when they search for information related to your products or services.

4. Generating Leads and Conversions

<u>Lead Magnet:</u> Content can be used as a lead magnet. Offering valuable content in exchange for contact information is a proven tactic for lead generation.

<u>Conversion Optimization:</u> Effective content encourages conversions by providing education and convincing potential customers of the value of your offering, which can lead directly to sales.

5. Encouraging Engagement and Interaction

<u>Building Relationships:</u> Content marketing provides opportunities to engage with your audience, whether through comments on your posts, shares on social media, or emails sent in response to newsletters.

<u>Community Building:</u> Over time, consistent, valuable content can help build a community around your brand, fostering loyalty and encouraging repeat business.

CHAPTER 3 Developing a Content Strategy

6. Cost-Effectiveness

Low Cost, High ROI: Compared to traditional forms of marketing, content marketing is relatively inexpensive but can produce significant returns in terms of brand visibility, customer engagement, and revenue.

Long-Term Value: The content you create can continue to engage customers, attract traffic, and generate leads long after it is initially published, offering an excellent return on investment.

7. Supporting Other Marketing Tactics

Multi-Channel Use: Content created for one purpose can be repurposed across multiple marketing channels, including social media, email marketing, and paid advertising, amplifying its reach and value.

Synergistic Effects: Content marketing works well with other marketing strategies, enhancing the effects of social media campaigns, email marketing efforts, and even paid advertising strategies.

CHAPTER 3 Developing a Content Strategy

TYPES OF CONTENT THAT ENGAGE AND CONVERT

The types of content that engage and convert are continually shifting. The algorithms are continually changing as the customers nowadays are continuously changing preferences and losing interest real quick. It's essential to focus on content types that not only capture attention but also encourage interaction and drive tangible results. It is crucial that your social media accounts to provide the customers reasons for which to follow you and then engage with you.

Here are some key content types that are particularly effective in engaging audiences and driving conversions:

1. Interactive Content
Types: Quizzes and polls on Instagram stories.

Benefits: By encouraging active participation, these interactive elements can enhance engagement rates, leading to increased visibility due to Instagram's engagement-favoring algorithm. They provide immediate and fun ways for users to interact with content, which not only helps in gathering data on user preferences and segmenting audiences but also enhances community building by making users feel valued.

Additionally, quizzes and polls diversify content offerings and can be integrated into broader marketing campaigns to support specific calls to action, such as visiting websites or participating in promotions. This interaction not only keeps the audience engaged but also helps brands stay relevant and connected with their followers, ultimately fostering loyalty and driving conversions.

CHAPTER 3 — Developing a Content Strategy

Benefits: UGC serves as authentic social proof, where potential customers see real people endorsing a product or service rather than corporate advertising. Also, seeing real experiences from actual customers reduces skepticism and builds greater trust in the brand. This type of validation from peers significantly enhances credibility.

6. Educational Content

Types:
- Tutorials: Step-by-step instructions or demonstrations designed to teach users how to perform specific tasks or use products effectively.
    - Use Case: Video tutorials on YouTube showing how to install software, or blog posts with detailed instructions on setting up a home network.

- E-courses: Structured digital courses that provide comprehensive coverage on particular topics, often segmented into modules or lessons.
    - Use Case: Online platforms offering multi-session courses on everything from photography to digital marketing, complete with assignments, assessments, and certificates.

- Webinars: Live or pre-recorded seminars conducted over the internet, allowing real-time interaction between the presenter and the audience.
    - Use Case: Live sessions hosted by industry experts discussing current trends, new technologies, or providing deep dives into specific topics.

CHAPTER 3   Developing a Content Strategy

- Detailed Guides: In-depth resources that cover a topic comprehensively, offering valuable insights and practical advice.
  - Use Case: Extensive PDF guides on best practices for SEO, or interactive online guides that walk users through complex legal or technical processes.

Benefits:
Providing valuable information that helps solve problems or improve skills can establish a brand as a thought leader, building trust and encouraging conversions through respect and authority. This strategic positioning not only enhances the brand's credibility but also fosters deeper customer engagement by delivering content that directly addresses their needs and solves their problems. As consumers recognize the brand's expertise, they are more likely to become loyal advocates, spreading word-of-mouth recommendations that further amplify the brand's reach. Ultimately, educational content serves as a cornerstone for sustainable business growth, turning informed users into long-term customers.

7. Podcasts

Types:
- Interview Series: Features conversations with guests such as industry experts, celebrities, or internal team members.
  - Use Case: A tech company might host a series where they interview innovators and thought leaders in the tech industry, providing insights and inspiration to listeners.

- Industry News: Regular updates and commentary on recent events and developments within a specific industry.
  - Use Case: A financial advisory firm could produce a weekly podcast that breaks down complex financial news into understandable insights for everyday investors.

CHAPTER 3 Developing a Content Strategy

- Educational Content: Focused on teaching listeners about specific topics, often involving tutorials, step-by-step guides, or deep dives into specialized subjects.
    - Use Case: A marketing agency might create a podcast series that teaches small business owners about basic to advanced marketing strategies in a structured format.

<u>Benefits:</u> Podcasts perfectly meet the needs of today's busy lifestyles, allowing people to listen while commuting, exercising, or performing other tasks. This format is particularly appealing due to exactly this versatility and accessibility, allowing listeners to engage with content while multitasking on a daily basis. Podcasts create an intimate communication channel where hosts can directly converse with their audience, establishing trust and loyalty that are essential for nurturing long-term relationships with listeners.

Furthermore, the audio format allows for flexibility in content delivery—from detailed educational sessions to casual interviews—making it easier to cater to diverse audience preferences and enhance the overall reach and impact of marketing efforts.

8. Visual Data
<u>Types:</u>
- Infographics: Comprehensive visuals that combine graphics, charts, and minimal text to explain topics, summarize data, and present patterns.
    - Platforms: Can be shared as static images on platforms like Facebook, Twitter, LinkedIn, or as detailed images on Pinterest.

CHAPTER 3 | Developing a Content Strategy

- Data Visualizations: Visual representations of data designed to surface patterns, trends, and outliers. Includes bar charts, line graphs, heat maps, and more.
    - Platforms: Ideal for inclusion in blog posts or reports, and shareable across all social media platforms, especially useful in interactive formats on websites.

- Dynamic Charts: Interactive charts that allow users to manipulate variables to see different data visualizations or outcomes.
    - Platforms: Best used on websites or in interactive digital reports where user engagement can lead to deeper insights.

Benefits: By transforming complex data into visually appealing and easily understandable formats, it enhances the accessibility of detailed information, making it less intimidating and more digestible for a broader audience. This simplification helps in quickly conveying key insights and value, which increases the content's shareability across social platforms, thereby boosting reach and engagement.

Additionally, visual data not only attracts more site traffic but also encourages deeper interaction with content, leading to higher conversion rates as users are better able to grasp and evaluate the benefits of a product or service.

CHAPTER 3 | **Developing a Content Strategy**

9. Storytelling
<u>Types:</u>
- Brand Stories
  - Description: These stories articulate the brand's history, mission, and the values that stand at its core. They often cover the genesis of the company, challenges faced, and the vision driving its future.
  - Example: A brand story might detail how a company was founded to address a particular market need or to uphold sustainability in all its operations, resonating with eco-conscious consumers.

- Customer Journey Stories
  - Description: These narratives focus on the customer's perspective, detailing their challenges and how the brand's product or service has transformed their lives.
  - Example: Customer journey stories may involve a detailed account of a customer who overcame significant challenges with the help of a product, showcasing the product's impact and the customer's satisfaction.

- Content that Narrates a Compelling Narrative
  - Description: This includes various forms of content like articles, videos, and podcasts that tell specific stories related to the brand, its products, or its community.
  - Example: A series of podcast episodes that share stories of how real users have implemented a product in innovative ways to improve their business operations or personal lives.

CHAPTER 3 Developing a Content Strategy

<u>Benefits:</u> Storytelling in digital marketing harnesses the power of emotional connection, making brands more relatable and memorable by sharing human-centric narratives. This approach taps into the psychological preference of people wanting to interact with other humans rather than faceless businesses. Stories evoke emotions and foster a personal connection, which significantly enhances brand recall and loyalty. By articulating customer journeys and brand histories, storytelling sets a brand apart, giving it a unique identity that resonates deeply with its audience. This emotional engagement drives conversions by influencing decision-making, as consumers are more likely to commit to brands that they feel emotionally connected to and trust.

Furthermore, storytelling transforms customers into brand advocates, as they share compelling narratives within their own networks, amplifying the brand's reach and impact organically.

10. SEO-Optimized Content
<u>Types:</u>
- Blog Posts
    - Description: In-depth posts that cover specific topics within an industry, providing valuable information or insights to readers.
    - Example: A blog post for a gardening website might focus on "Tips for Winter Plant Care," incorporating keywords related to winter gardening tips.
- Articles
    - Description: Longer pieces that explore subjects comprehensively, often used to establish authority and depth in a subject matter.
    - Example: An extensive article on a tech website about "Emerging AI Technologies in 2024" that includes key phrases trending in the tech industry.

CHAPTER 3 Developing a Content Strategy

- Landing Pages
    - Description: Strategically designed pages tailored to specific marketing campaigns or audience segments, focusing on converting visitors into leads or customers.
    - Example: A landing page for a digital marketing service might target the keyword "Best SEO services for small businesses" and provide compelling reasons to choose the service, along with clear calls to action.

Benefits: SEO-optimized content is crucial for enhancing a website's visibility, attracting more organic traffic, and improving engagement and conversion rates. By tailoring content to align with specific search queries, it not only ranks higher in search engine results but also addresses the direct needs and questions of the audience, making it highly relevant and engaging. This strategic alignment helps in building credibility and trust, as websites that appear at the top of search results are often perceived as more authoritative.

Moreover, SEO-optimized content is a cost-effective marketing strategy, providing sustainable traffic without the ongoing costs associated with paid advertising. Once established, well-optimized content can continue to attract visitors and generate leads or sales for an extended period, offering long-term benefits from a single investment in quality content creation.

Based on your customer personas you create, you can leverage a mix of these content types, tailored to the specific preferences and behaviors of your target audience. The key is to stay adaptive, monitor performance, and continuously refine your content strategy based on analytics and feedback to continuously drive engagement and converting leads into customers.

CHAPTER 3 Developing a Content Strategy

CRAFTING QUALITY CONTENT: BEST PRACTICES

Content is everywhere. Just think of all of the accounts on Instagram. They all share content. You need to differentiate yourself somehow. In a digital world saturated with information, the challenge isn't just creating content; it's creating content that stands out. As businesses and individuals compete for attention in an ever-expanding online universe, the need to produce content that is not only engaging and informative but also distinct and memorable becomes paramount.

Understand Your Audience
- Deep Audience Insights: Before you start creating content, it's crucial to have a deep understanding of your audience. Research their preferences, pain points, and behaviors to tailor your content to meet their needs and expectations.

- Personas: Develop detailed buyer personas that outline the characteristics, goals, and challenges of your ideal customers. This helps in crafting messages that resonate personally with your audience.

Define Clear Objectives
- Purpose-Driven Content: Each piece of content should have a clear purpose. Whether it's to inform, entertain, persuade, or convert, defining the objective will guide the content creation process and help measure its success.

- Align with Business Goals: Ensure that the content supports your overall business objectives, such as increasing brand awareness, boosting sales, or enhancing customer loyalty.

CHAPTER 3 — Developing a Content Strategy

Focus on High-Quality Writing
- Clarity and Coherence: Use a clear and concise writing style to ensure that your message is easily understandable. Avoid jargon unless your audience is familiar with it.

- Grammar and Style: Invest in good editing practices. Use tools like Grammarly or Hemingway to check for grammatical errors and readability.

Optimize for SEO
- Keyword Research: Incorporate relevant keywords naturally into your content to boost its visibility in search results. Use keywords that your target audience is searching for.

- On-Page SEO Techniques: Beyond keywords, optimize your content with meta descriptions, proper tagging, and structured data to improve SEO performance.

Make It Engaging
- Interactive Elements: Include interactive elements like polls, quizzes, or clickable slideshows to keep the audience engaged.

- Visuals: Break up text with high-quality images, videos, or infographics. Visual aids not only make the content more appealing but also help in explaining complex information.

Provide Real Value
- Educational Content: Offer actionable advice, step-by-step guides, or insightful analyses. Content should provide real value to the reader and not just serve as a vessel for keywords.

- Unique Insights: Share unique perspectives or data to stand out from the content available from competitors. Original insights establish thought leadership.

CHAPTER 3 — Developing a Content Strategy

Consistency Is Key
- Brand Voice: Maintain a consistent brand voice across all content to strengthen brand identity. Whether professional or conversational, the voice should reflect your brand personality.

- Regular Updates: Keep your content fresh and relevant by updating it regularly. This is especially important for evergreen content and high-performing articles.

Promote and Measure
- Distribution Strategy: Creating great content is only the first step; having a solid distribution strategy is crucial. Use social media, email newsletters, and other channels to promote your content.

- Analytics: Continuously measure the performance of your content through analytics. Look at engagement metrics such as time on page, bounce rate, and conversions to understand what works and refine your strategy accordingly.

Cross-Promotion
Utilize your content across multiple channels. For example, promote a blog post on social media, summarize it in an email newsletter, or discuss it in a podcast episode. This increases the reach and lifespan of your content.

CHAPTER 3: Developing a Content Strategy

Repurpose your content

Maximizing the reach and utility of your content by adapting and repurposing it for different formats and platforms is an efficient and effective strategy. A single piece of content, such as a blog article, can be transformed into multiple pieces across various media. For example, key points from an article can be converted into an engaging email newsletter, visual posts for social media, concise stories for platforms like Instagram or Facebook, or even expanded into a detailed press release. This approach not only extends the life of the original content but also ensures that it reaches different segments of your audience, who may prefer different types of media. Repurposing content can significantly increase your marketing efficiency and effectiveness by reinforcing your message and increasing its exposure without requiring a proportional increase in time and resources.

CHAPTER 4

Using customer journey mapping to refine marketing efforts

Customer journey mapping is a strategic approach to understanding the steps your customers take from becoming aware of your brand to making a purchase and beyond. This visual representation of the customer's experience provides valuable insights into customer interactions and pain points, allowing for optimization of the strategies and touchpoints across the entire journey.

1. Building the Map

Gather Data
The initial step in building a customer journey map is to collect comprehensive data that reflects how customers interact with your brand across various touchpoints.

Sources of Data:
- Website Analytics: Tools like Google Analytics provide insights into how users navigate your site, the pages they linger on, and where they drop off.
- CRM Systems: Customer Relationship Management systems offer valuable data on customer interactions, sales transactions, and service histories.
- Customer Surveys: Direct feedback from customers can unveil perceptions and pain points experienced during their journey.
- Social Media Interactions: Analyzing comments, shares, and other engagement forms on platforms like Facebook, Instagram, and Twitter can reveal how customers feel about your brand in a public forum.

CHAPTER 4: Using customer journey mapping to refine marketing efforts

Objective: Use this collected data to understand critical paths and actions taken by customers, identify common issues they face, and highlight moments of delight or frustration.

Identify Key Stages

Stages of the Journey:
- Awareness: The customer becomes aware of your brand through various channels such as advertising, word-of-mouth, or organic search.
- Consideration: The customer evaluates your offerings by comparing with competitors or diving deeper into your product's features.
- Decision: Decisions are made on whether to purchase based on the information gathered in the previous stages.
- Purchase: The actual transaction takes place.
- Post-Purchase: Includes customer service interactions, loyalty programs, and potential advocacy or churn.

Purpose: Clearly defining these stages helps in pinpointing where customers might feel satisfied or encounter obstacles. Each stage should address specific goals and the mindset of the customer, enhancing the focus on delivering targeted messages and interventions.

Using customer journey mapping to refine marketing efforts

Visual Representation: Create a visual map using tools like Lucidchart, Microsoft Visio, Miro, or simple whiteboarding.

Developing the Map:
- Layout: Arrange the stages of the customer journey from left to right or in a circular pattern to represent the cycle nature of customer engagement.
- Incorporate Emotions: Alongside each stage, note the emotional responses customers are likely to experience, such as frustration, joy, or disappointment.
- Interaction Points: Highlight specific interactions within each stage, like clicking an ad, calling customer service, or receiving a follow-up email.
- Insights and Opportunities: Attach insights gained from the data and identify opportunities for improvement at each stage.

Objective: The visual map should serve as a clear and comprehensive guide that outlines the customer journey in a way that is easily understandable and actionable for all stakeholders involved in customer experience management.

2. Identifying Pain Points and Opportunities

Analyze Interactions: This step involves a deep dive into the interactions customers have with your brand at each stage of their journey. The goal is to uncover any obstacles or frustrations that might deter a customer's progress or satisfaction.

Methods:
- Customer Feedback Analysis: Systematically review customer feedback across all touchpoints to identify recurring themes or complaints.
- Session Replays and Heatmaps: Utilize tools like Hotjar or Crazy Egg to visually see how users interact with your website, identifying areas where users seem to struggle or abandon the journey.

CHAPTER 4: Using customer journey mapping to refine marketing efforts

- Performance Metrics Review: Assess performance indicators such as bounce rates, conversion rates, and average time on page to pinpoint stages where customers are losing interest or encountering problems.

Common Issues:
- Website Navigation Difficulties: Complex or unintuitive navigation that confuses customers.
- Inadequate Product Information: Lack of sufficient detail that may prevent a customer from making an informed decision.
- Delayed Customer Service Responses: Slow response times leading to customer frustration and potential loss of sale.

Highlight Moments of Truth = are pivotal points in the customer journey where a customer's decision to continue or abandon their path is made. These are critical opportunities to convert interest into action.

Identification Process:
- Journey Analytics: Use your customer journey map to identify stages with high dropout rates.
- Customer Surveys and Interviews: Directly ask customers about their decision-making process to understand what factors influenced their decisions at critical points.

Strategic Importance:
- Enhancing these key moments can drastically improve customer retention and conversion rates. For instance, simplifying the checkout process can reduce cart abandonment, while proactive customer support at the decision stage can increase conversions.

CHAPTER 4 — Using customer journey mapping to refine marketing efforts

Opportunity Identification

Utilizing Insights:
- From Pain Points: Each identified pain point is an opportunity to innovate or improve. For example, if customers find the website hard to navigate, consider a redesign that simplifies the user interface.
- From Moments of Truth: Enhance these moments by ensuring that all possible customer needs are addressed promptly and effectively. For instance, offer live chat support during business hours to help customers immediately during the decision phase.

Broadening the Scope:
- Product Offerings: Look for gaps in your product range or service features that, if addressed, could satisfy an unmet need.
- Customer Engagement Strategies: Develop new engagement strategies such as personalized emails, loyalty programs, or community-building activities based on customer interests and behaviors.

Implementation:
- Pilot Projects: Test new ideas through limited-time offers or small-scale launches to measure effectiveness before a full rollout.
- Continuous Feedback Loop: Establish a system for ongoing feedback to keep your strategies responsive to customer needs and market changes.

Using customer journey mapping to refine marketing efforts

3. Aligning Marketing Strategies

Personalization: Personalization involves crafting marketing messages that resonate with the customer at various stages of their journey, based on their unique needs, preferences, and behaviors.

Application:
- Awareness Stage: At this initial contact point, use engaging and broadly appealing content to attract attention. This might include educational blog posts, engaging videos, and eye-catching infographics that introduce your brand and values.
- Consideration Stage: Provide more detailed content that helps customers evaluate your offerings against their needs. This could involve comparison guides, customer testimonials, and detailed product descriptions.
- Decision Stage: Use personalized emails or retargeting ads that remind customers of the items they viewed or left in their cart, featuring promotions or limited-time offers to encourage conversion.

Benefits: Personalization increases relevance and engagement, reduces customer churn, and enhances the likelihood of conversion by delivering the right message at the right time.

Channel Optimization: Channel optimization entails selecting and prioritizing marketing channels based on their effectiveness at each stage of the customer journey.

Strategy Implementation:
- Identify Channels: Determine which channels (social media, email, direct mail, online ads, etc.) most effectively reach your customers at each stage. For instance, social media might be most effective at the awareness stage, while email might be better for direct engagement at the decision stage.

CHAPTER 4 — Using customer journey mapping to refine marketing efforts

- Optimize Spend: Allocate budget according to the channels' performance, focusing on those that offer the highest ROI in terms of engagement and conversions.
- Continual Assessment: Regularly analyze channel performance. Adjust strategies as needed to respond to changes in consumer behavior or channel effectiveness.
- Benefits: Optimizing channels ensures that marketing efforts are not wasted on platforms that do not reach your audience effectively, thereby increasing overall campaign efficiency and effectiveness.

Feedback Loops: Feedback loops are crucial for maintaining the relevance and effectiveness of your marketing strategies. They allow for continuous learning and adaptation based on direct customer insights.

Implementing Feedback Loops:
- Customer Surveys: Conduct regular surveys to gather insights directly from your customers about their experiences and satisfaction levels at different journey stages.
- Social Media Monitoring: Use social listening tools to track mentions, comments, and discussions about your brand, providing real-time feedback on customer sentiments.
- Analytics: Utilize analytics tools to measure engagement and conversion rates across different channels and content types. This data can highlight what's working and what isn't.
- Review and Adjust: Regularly review customer feedback and analytics data to identify trends and issues. Use this information to refine your marketing strategies, making necessary adjustments to messages, channels, and tactics.

Benefits: Establishing robust feedback loops ensures that your marketing strategies remain aligned with customer expectations and market dynamics, enabling quicker responsiveness to changes and opportunities for improvement.

Using customer journey mapping to refine marketing efforts

4. Implementation and Iteration

Cross-Functional Collaboration: Effective customer journey mapping requires insights from various facets of the organization to ensure a holistic view of the customer experience. This involves integrating input from marketing, sales, customer service, and even product development teams.

Process:
- Stakeholder Meetings: Organize regular meetings with representatives from all relevant departments to gather diverse perspectives on the customer journey.
- Shared Responsibility: Assign specific roles to different departments, such as sales focusing on decision and purchase stages, while customer service provides insights into post-purchase experiences.
- Unified Vision: Align all departments under a common goal of enhancing customer satisfaction and loyalty, ensuring that every touchpoint along the customer journey is optimized for consistency and effectiveness.

Benefits: Collaborating across functions ensures that the journey map reflects a complete view of the customer experience, leading to more accurate and actionable insights. It also fosters a sense of ownership and accountability across the organization.

Test and Learn: The dynamic nature of customer interactions and preferences necessitates a flexible approach to marketing strategies. Utilizing A/B testing and pilot programs allows for experimenting with new ideas on a small scale before full implementation.

Methodology:
- A/B Testing: Implement A/B testing to compare two versions of a campaign or touchpoint to determine which performs better in terms of customer engagement and conversion rates.

CHAPTER 4: Using customer journey mapping to refine marketing efforts

- Pilot Programs: Launch new initiatives in controlled environments or selected markets to test their effectiveness and gather detailed feedback.
- Analytics and Feedback: Use analytical tools and customer feedback to evaluate the success of tests and pilots, focusing on key performance indicators relevant to the objectives.

<u>Benefits:</u> This test-and-learn approach minimizes risk by allowing adjustments to be made based on empirical data and real-world feedback, ensuring that only the most effective strategies are rolled out widely.

Regular Updates: As markets evolve and customer behaviors change, the customer journey map must also adapt to stay relevant. Regular updates ensure that the map accurately represents current customer experiences and expectations.

<u>Updating Process:</u>
- Review Cycles: Establish regular intervals (e.g., quarterly, bi-annually) for reviewing and updating the journey map.
- Incorporate New Data: Continuously integrate new customer data and insights into the journey map. This includes feedback from recent marketing campaigns, changes in customer service interactions, and shifts in market conditions.
- Change Management: Ensure changes to the journey map are communicated effectively across the organization and that updates are reflected in related processes and strategies.

<u>Benefits:</u> Regularly updating the journey map ensures that marketing and customer service strategies remain aligned with actual customer needs and behaviors, enhancing the ability to deliver exceptional customer experiences and drive loyalty.

CHAPTER 4 — Using customer journey mapping to refine marketing efforts

5. Leveraging Technology

Automation Tools: Marketing automation tools are crucial for streamlining complex marketing campaigns and personalizing interactions with customers at scale.

Implementation:
- Tool Selection: Choose automation platforms that integrate seamlessly with your existing CRM systems and digital marketing tools. Popular options include HubSpot, Marketo, and Salesforce Pardot.
- Personalized Messaging: Use these tools to automate and personalize email campaigns, social media posts, and other communications based on where customers are in their journey. For instance, trigger welcome emails when a new user signs up or abandonment emails when a cart is not completed.
- Campaign Management: Automate repetitive tasks such as posting on social media at optimal times, segmenting email lists based on user behavior, and managing content across different platforms.

Benefits: Automation allows for consistent and timely interactions with customers, reduces the likelihood of human error, and frees up marketing teams to focus on more strategic tasks. Personalized messages ensure relevance, which can increase customer engagement and move them smoothly along the customer journey.

Analytics and AI: Advanced analytics and artificial intelligence are transforming how businesses understand and interact with their customers by providing deeper insights and predictive capabilities.

Implementation:
- Data Integration: Aggregate data from various sources such as web traffic, social media interactions, purchase history, and customer feedback to create a comprehensive view of the customer journey.

Using customer journey mapping to refine marketing efforts

- AI Tools: Implement AI-driven analytics tools like IBM Watson, Google Analytics AI, or Adobe Analytics to analyze large data sets quickly and identify patterns that may not be visible to human analysts.
- Predictive Analytics: Use AI to predict future customer behaviors based on their past interactions. This can help anticipate needs and preferences, allowing for proactive rather than reactive marketing strategies.
- Segmentation and Personalization: Leverage AI to refine customer segmentation by identifying nuanced behavioral and demographic patterns, enabling hyper-personalized marketing strategies.

Benefits: Analytics and AI enhance the accuracy of your customer journey mapping by providing real-time insights and predictive analysis. This enables a more dynamic approach to marketing, where strategies can be adjusted almost instantaneously based on the latest data. AI's predictive power also allows for more effective targeting, reducing marketing waste and increasing ROI.

e.g. Customer Journey Map for an Online Makeup Store

1. Awareness Stage
- How Customers Discover You: Potential customers become aware of your brand through targeted social media ads on platforms like Instagram and Facebook, influencer partnerships, and beauty blogs.
- Key Actions: Viewing ads, reading posts, and watching sponsored content.
- Goal: Increase brand visibility and spark interest.

Using customer journey mapping to refine marketing efforts

2. Consideration Stage
- Research and Evaluation: After becoming aware of the brand, customers move into the consideration phase where they start researching the products. They read reviews on your website and third-party sites, watch tutorial videos using your products, and compare prices and features against competitors.
- Key Actions: Visiting product pages, reading customer testimonials, and comparing different products.
- Goal: Provide enough information to assist in their decision-making process.

3. Decision Stage
- Decision Making: Customers decide which products to purchase. This decision is often influenced by promotions, product availability, and final evaluations of product benefits.
- Key Actions: Adding items to the shopping cart, applying discount codes.
- Goal: Make the checkout process as seamless as possible to convert interest into a purchase.

4. Purchase Stage
- Buying the Product: The customer completes the purchase through a streamlined online checkout system. Payment options are flexible, and security is emphasized to reassure the customer.
- Key Actions: Entering payment information, choosing delivery options.
- Goal: Ensure a smooth transaction to reduce cart abandonment and increase conversion rates.

CHAPTER 4 — Using customer journey mapping to refine marketing efforts

5. Post-Purchase Stage
- Follow-Up and Retention: After the purchase, the focus shifts to keeping the customer satisfied and engaged. Customers receive an order confirmation email immediately after purchase, followed by a shipment tracking email.
- Key Actions: Reviewing the product online, engaging with post-purchase follow-up emails that may include requests for feedback, offers for related products, or loyalty program benefits.
- Goal: Enhance customer satisfaction and foster long-term loyalty. Encourage repeat purchases and collect valuable feedback to improve products and services.

Throughout all stages, personalized email marketing plays a critical role in guiding the customer through the journey. Retargeting ads and continuous engagement on social media also help in maintaining interest and encouraging repeat visits and purchases.

HOW TO CREATE A CUSTOMER JOURNEY MAP FOR A START-UP?

Building a Customer Journey Map for a startup business involves a blend of customer insights, assumptions based on your target audience, and iterative learning. Since startups may not have a wealth of historical customer data, leveraging customer personas becomes a vital starting point. Here's a step-by-step guide on how to build a Customer Journey Map for a startup:

1. Define Your Customer Personas
Start by creating detailed customer personas. These are semi-fictional characters that represent your ideal customers. They should include demographic details, behaviors, motivations, goals, and pain points. The development of these personas should be based on any available data, market research, and educated assumptions. Personas help you hypothesize how different types of customers will interact with your service/product.

Using customer journey mapping to refine marketing efforts

2. Identify Touchpoints

Determine where your customers will interact with your business across multiple channels. Touchpoints could include social media interactions, website visits, customer service calls, email communications, and physical interactions if applicable. List these touchpoints for each stage of the customer journey: awareness, consideration, decision, purchase, and post-purchase.

3. Map the Customer Journey

Create a visual map that outlines the path each persona might take from first becoming aware of your product to post-purchase behaviors. For each stage of the journey, consider:

- Actions: What is the customer doing at this stage? For example, searching for solutions online, comparing prices, etc.
- Motivations: Why is the customer motivated to move to the next stage? What drives their decisions?
- Questions: What are the potential uncertainties or questions customers might have at this stage?
- Barriers: What obstacles might prevent customers from moving to the next stage?

4. Hypothesize and Validate

Since startups may lack extensive real-world data, initial journey maps will be based largely on assumptions that need to be validated. Set up mechanisms to test and refine these assumptions as you gather real customer data. This can be done through:

- Customer Feedback: Directly ask customers for feedback through surveys, interviews, or usability testing.
- Analytics: Use website and social media analytics to understand how customers are actually behaving compared to how you assumed they would.
- A/B Testing: Experiment with different approaches in your marketing and sales processes to see what works best and adjust your journey map accordingly.

CHAPTER 4: Using customer journey mapping to refine marketing efforts

5. Adjust and Iterate
Customer journey maps should not be static; they need to evolve as you learn more about your customers and as your business grows. Regularly update the map based on new insights and make sure that it reflects any changes in your business strategy, market conditions, or customer feedback.

6. Integrate Across the Organization
Ensure that insights from the customer journey map are shared across your organization. Every department, from marketing and sales to product development and customer service, should understand the map and how their role impacts the customer experience.

Building a Customer Journey Map as a startup involves making educated guesses about your customers, testing those assumptions, and refining your approach based on data. It's a dynamic tool that helps align your startup's efforts with customer expectations and enhances the overall strategic approach to market entry and growth.

CHAPTER 5

Building a Scalable Digital Marketing Ecosystem

SUSTAINABLE STRATEGIES FOR GROWTH

For businesses aiming to sustain long-term growth, it's crucial to establish a scalable digital marketing ecosystem. This involves implementing strategies that are not only effective in the short term but also adaptable and resilient to market changes and business scaling. This section will outline key sustainable strategies for growth within such an ecosystem.

1. Integrated Digital Infrastructure

A robust digital infrastructure that integrates various marketing tools and platforms is foundational to scaling operations efficiently.

Implementation:
- Technology Stack: Invest in a cohesive technology stack that includes marketing automation, CRM, analytics, and content management systems that work seamlessly together.
- Cloud-Based Solutions: Utilize cloud services to ensure scalability and flexibility, allowing for easy expansion as the business grows and market demands shift.

Benefits: An integrated infrastructure reduces redundancies, improves data flow across different marketing channels, and provides a single source of truth for measuring marketing effectiveness.

CHAPTER 5: Building a Scalable Digital Marketing Ecosystem

2. Data-Driven Decision Making

Building a culture of data-driven decision making is essential for sustainable growth.

Implementation:
- **Comprehensive Data Collection:** Continuously collect data across all customer touchpoints to gain a holistic view of the customer journey.
- **Advanced Analytics:** Use advanced data analytics and business intelligence tools to derive actionable insights from complex data sets.

Benefits: Leveraging data helps in making informed marketing decisions, optimizing campaigns in real-time, and predicting future trends that can inform long-term strategy.

3. Agile Marketing Practices

Adopting agile practices allows marketing teams to be more responsive and adaptable to changes in the market.

Implementation:
- **Sprint Planning:** Implement sprint cycles to plan, execute, and review marketing experiments and campaigns.
- **Cross-functional Teams:** Foster collaboration across marketing, sales, product development, and customer service teams to enhance creativity and rapid problem-solving.

Benefits: Agile marketing enhances responsiveness to customer needs and market changes, enabling quicker pivots and continuous improvement of marketing efforts.

CHAPTER 5: Building a Scalable Digital Marketing Ecosystem

4. Customer-Centric Approach

At the heart of sustainable growth strategies is a relentless focus on customer satisfaction and engagement.

Implementation:
- Customer Feedback Loops: Establish mechanisms to regularly gather and analyze customer feedback.
- Personalization: Utilize technology to deliver personalized experiences at scale, tailored to the preferences and behaviors of individual customers.

Benefits: A customer-centric approach not only improves customer loyalty and retention but also drives word-of-mouth marketing which is crucial for organic growth.

5. Continuous Learning and Innovation

The digital landscape is constantly evolving, and sustaining growth requires a commitment to learning and innovation.

Implementation:
- Ongoing Training: Regularly update the skills and knowledge of your marketing team through training and professional development opportunities.
- R&D for Marketing: Invest in research and development specifically for marketing to explore new tools, technologies, and methodologies.

Benefits: Staying at the forefront of digital marketing innovations ensures the business remains competitive and is able to capitalize on new opportunities for growth.

CHAPTER 5 — Building a Scalable Digital Marketing Ecosystem

6. Eco-friendly Marketing

Integrating sustainability into marketing not only appeals to increasingly environmentally conscious consumers but also ensures compliance with emerging regulations.

Implementation:
- Sustainable Practices: Adopt eco-friendly practices in digital marketing efforts, such as optimizing digital asset sizes to reduce energy consumption and prioritizing digital over physical marketing materials.

Benefits: Sustainable marketing practices can enhance brand reputation, attract like-minded consumers, and contribute to the global effort of reducing environmental impact.

MEASURING SUCCESS & MAKING ADJUSTMENTS

Introduction to Measurement and Adjustment For small business owners implementing digital marketing strategies, measuring success and making necessary adjustments is critical. This process ensures that your marketing efforts are effective, providing the best return on investment and continuously enhancing your engagement with customers.

1. Setting Key Performance Indicators (KPIs)

Key Performance Indicators are metrics that help you gauge the success of your marketing strategies against your predefined objectives.

Implementation:
- Identify Business Goals: Define what success looks like for your business, whether it's increasing sales, generating leads, enhancing brand awareness, or improving customer retention.
- Choose Relevant KPIs: Select KPIs that directly reflect progress towards your goals. For example, if your goal is to enhance online sales, relevant KPIs might include conversion rates, average order value, and cart abandonment rates.

Building a Scalable Digital Marketing Ecosystem

Benefits: Having clear KPIs allows you to track performance effectively and identify areas that need improvement.

2. Utilizing Analytics Tools

Digital analytics tools can provide detailed insights into how your marketing efforts are performing and how users are interacting with your content and platforms.

Implementation:
- Tools Selection: Choose analytics tools that fit your business size and complexity. Google Analytics is a comprehensive, free tool that provides insights into website traffic, user behavior, and conversion metrics. Social media platforms also offer built-in analytics that provides data on engagement and reach.
- Regular Monitoring: Set a routine to regularly check these metrics. This could be weekly or monthly, depending on your business activity level.

Benefits: Regular use of analytics tools helps you understand the effectiveness of your marketing campaigns and website performance, guiding you in optimizing both.

3. Conducting A/B Testing

A/B testing involves comparing two versions of a webpage, email, or other marketing asset to determine which one performs better in terms of your KPIs.

Implementation:
- Test Design: Develop two versions (A and B) of a marketing asset with one key variable changed, such as the call-to-action text, layout, or images used.
- Segment Audience: Divide your audience randomly to ensure each segment is statistically similar and expose them to different versions.
- Analyze Results: Measure which version achieves better performance in terms of predefined metrics.

Building a Scalable Digital Marketing Ecosystem

Benefits: A/B testing removes guesswork from decision-making, allowing you to make data-driven choices that can improve the effectiveness of your marketing efforts.

4. Reviewing and Adjusting Strategies
The digital landscape is dynamic, with customer preferences and competitive environments constantly evolving.

Implementation:
- Feedback Integration: Incorporate customer feedback to understand their experience and expectations better. This can be gathered through surveys, reviews, or direct customer interactions.
- Strategy Adjustment: Based on the analysis and feedback, refine your marketing strategies. This might mean adjusting your content, switching up your advertising channels, or revising your user interface.

Benefits: Regularly updating your strategies in response to feedback and performance metrics ensures that your marketing efforts remain relevant and effective, maximizing ROI and customer satisfaction.

KPIs

Setting and monitoring Key Performance Indicators (KPIs) are vital for measuring the success of your marketing efforts and ensuring that you are on track to achieve your business goals. Here's a detailed guide on how to select KPIs, set them, and effectively monitor them:

Examples of KPIs

1. Website Traffic
Measures the number of visitors to your website. Useful for gauging the effectiveness of your content marketing and SEO strategies.

 **Building a Scalable Digital Marketing Ecosystem**

2. Conversion Rate

The percentage of visitors who complete a desired action (such as filling out a form, signing up for a newsletter, or making a purchase). This KPI is critical for understanding the effectiveness of your website and landing pages in compelling user actions.

For e-commerce, an average conversion rate is about 1-2%. For B2B companies, especially on lead generation forms, the average can be around 2.5-3%.

Conversion Rate = (Total Number of Visitors / Number of Conversions) × 100

3. Customer Acquisition Cost (CAC)

The total cost of acquiring a new customer, calculated by dividing total marketing expenses by the number of new customers. This is essential for evaluating the efficiency of your marketing spend.

This heavily depends on the industry and the lifetime value of customers. Generally, a CAC that is one-third or less of the Customer Lifetime Value (CLTV) is considered healthy.

Formula: Customer Acquisition Cost = Number of New Customers Acquired / Total Marketing Expenses

4. Customer Lifetime Value (CLTV)

The total revenue a business can reasonably expect from a single customer account throughout their relationship with the company. This helps in determining how much to invest in acquiring new customers and retaining existing ones.

A good CLTV to CAC ratio is 3:1, meaning the lifetime value of a customer should be three times the cost of acquiring them.

CLTV = Average Order Value × Number of Repeat Sales × Average Retention Time

CHAPTER 5: Building a Scalable Digital Marketing Ecosystem

5. Engagement Rate

Commonly used for social media, this measures interactions like shares, likes, and comments relative to your total number of followers. It helps assess how engaging your content is.

Varies by platform but generally:
- Facebook: typical around 0.08% - 0.09%, good from 0.1% to 0.2% (keep in mind that the Facebook algorithm works like this: as the number of followers increase, the engagement rate decreases. For smaller audiences, these ranges can be higher).
- Instagram: Higher engagement, between 1% and 3%
- Twitter: Typically lower, around 0.045%
- LinkedIn: around 0.2% to 0.5% (Content related to business, professional development, and company updates tends to perform well.)
- TikTok: from 3% to 9%
- YouTube: around 4% to 6%

6. Email Open and Click-through Rates

Indicates how many people on an email list open an email and then click on a link within the email. These metrics are vital for assessing email campaign effectiveness.

Open Rate:
- Average: About 15-25% across industries.
- Good Rate: Above 20% is generally good.

Click-through Rate:
- Average: Around 2.5%.
- Good Rate: Higher than 3% is often considered effective.

7. Click-Through Rate (CTR)

Measures the percentage of people who click on a link or ad after seeing it. It helps assess the effectiveness of online advertisements or email campaigns.

CTR = (Number of Clicks / Number of Impressions) × 100

CHAPTER 5
Building a Scalable Digital Marketing Ecosystem

8. Return on Investment (ROI)
Evaluates the efficiency and profitability of an investment compared to its cost. In marketing, ROI helps measure the effectiveness of various marketing campaigns in generating revenue relative to the amount spent on those campaigns. Strategies with a high ROI should be prioritized and potentially expanded.

ROI = (Cost of Investment / Net Profit) × 100

9. Bounce Rate
Indicates the percentage of visitors who navigate away from the site after viewing only one page. A high bounce rate can suggest that site content is not relevant or engaging.

<u>Average Bounce Rates by Type of Site</u>
- Retail or E-commerce Sites: Typically see bounce rates between 20% to 45%. Lower bounce rates are usually better, as they indicate that visitors are engaging more deeply, likely viewing product details, reading descriptions, and checking out purchase options.
- B2B Websites: Can expect an average bounce rate of 30% to 60%. The wider range accounts for the variability in content type, from blogs to product-specific landing pages.
- Blogs: Often have higher bounce rates, ranging from 65% to 90%. This is because users may simply read a single article they were interested in and then leave.
- Landing Pages: With a specific call to action, especially those for direct marketing or advertising campaigns, might see bounce rates from 70% to 90%, depending on the nature of the campaign.
- Service Sites: Where users might be looking for a specific service or piece of contact information, bounce rates can range from 10% to 30%.

CHAPTER 5: Building a Scalable Digital Marketing Ecosystem

Bounce Rate = (Number of Single Page Visits / Total Visits) × 100

10. Email List Growth Rate

Tracks how quickly your email list is growing. Helps assess the effectiveness of lead generation efforts. Typically, a healthy email list growth rate is considered to be between 1% to 3% per month.

Email List Growth Rate = (Net New Subscribers / Total Number of Email List Subscribers at Start of Period) × 100

CONCLUSION

KEY TAKEAWAYS

1. Adaptability is Crucial: The digital world is ever-evolving, and staying adaptable—ready to tweak strategies in response to new technologies and changing consumer behaviors—is essential for continued success.

2. Data-Driven Decision Making: Emphasizing the importance of analytics and measurable outcomes, we've seen how data-driven decisions can refine your marketing efforts and maximize ROI.

3. Customer-Centric Approach: At the heart of all digital marketing efforts is the customer. A deep understanding of your target audience, personalized interactions, and consistently valuable content can foster lasting customer relationships.

4. Integrated Strategies: Combining various digital marketing techniques and channels—from SEO to social media and beyond—creates a cohesive and powerful marketing ecosystem that amplifies your brand's message across multiple platforms.

5. Content is King, but Context is Queen: While producing high-quality content is crucial, delivering it in the right context—where and when your audience will most appreciate it—significantly boosts its effectiveness. Understanding the customer's journey and their content consumption habits can help you tailor your content strategy effectively.

6. Social Proof and User-Generated Content: Encouraging and leveraging user-generated content (UGC) can enhance credibility and trustworthiness. Reviews, testimonials, and user-contributed images or videos can provide social proof and influence purchasing decisions of potential customers.

CONCLUSION

7. Cross-Channel Integration: To maximize the impact of your digital marketing efforts, integrate strategies across multiple channels. A cohesive message across your website, social media, email, and other digital platforms ensures a unified brand experience. This cross-channel integration supports a seamless customer journey, enhancing both acquisition and retention.

8. Leverage Video Content: The power of video content continues to grow, offering a compelling way to engage audiences. Videos can increase dwell time on your site, improve engagement rates on social media, and provide a versatile medium for explaining complex products or services. Incorporating video marketing into your strategy can enhance brand recall and customer interaction.

9. Building Personal Connections: Develop marketing strategies that focus on building personal connections with your audience. Personalized marketing helps in creating a more emotional connection with the audience, which can lead to higher loyalty and customer retention rates.

10. Strategic Use of KPIs for Enhanced Decision Making: Key Performance Indicators (KPIs) are essential for measuring the effectiveness of your digital marketing strategies. By identifying and tracking the right KPIs, you can gain valuable insights into the performance of your campaigns and make data-driven decisions to optimize them. Select KPIs that align closely with your business objectives and provide clear indicators of campaign success, such as conversion rates, engagement rates, and ROI. Regular monitoring and analysis of these KPIs not only help in assessing the efficiency of your marketing efforts but also guide strategic adjustments to improve outcomes and achieve your marketing goals more effectively.

CONCLUSION

LOOKING AHEAD

As we wrap up our exploration of digital marketing essentials, it's crucial to focus on the path forward and how to continue evolving with the rapidly changing digital landscape. The journey of mastering digital marketing does not end here. Instead, it requires ongoing commitment, adaptability, and foresight. Here's how you can stay proactive and innovative in your digital marketing efforts:

1. Embrace Emerging Technologies

- Stay Curious: Keep an eye on emerging technologies such as artificial intelligence (AI), augmented reality (AR), and virtual reality (VR). These technologies are beginning to play significant roles in personalizing and enhancing the customer experience.

- Experiment: Don't hesitate to experiment with new tools and platforms that can give you a competitive edge. For example, consider how chatbots could improve customer service or how blockchain technology might enhance data security and transparency in your campaigns.

2. Anticipate Market Trends

- Continuous Learning: The digital marketing arena is continuously influenced by changing consumer behaviors and technological advancements. Stay ahead by regularly engaging in professional development, whether through online courses, webinars, or industry conferences.

- Adapt Strategies: As market dynamics shift, so should your strategies. This might mean changing your content approach to match new consumer preferences or adjusting your ad spend based on the latest platform algorithms and advertising trends.

CONCLUSION

3. Foster a Culture of Innovation
- Encourage Creativity: Foster a work environment where new ideas are welcomed and experimentation is encouraged. This can lead to innovative strategies that set your brand apart.
- Iterative Improvements: Implement a culture of testing and iteration where campaigns are continuously refined based on performance data and feedback loops.

4. Sustainable Practices
- Long-term Focus: As digital marketing evolves, so does the importance of sustainability in business practices. Consider the environmental impact of your digital campaigns and strive to implement green marketing practices wherever possible.
- Ethical Marketing: Uphold high ethical standards in your marketing. This includes transparency about data usage, respecting user privacy, and avoiding manipulative tactics.

5. Build on Community and Social Impact
- Engagement Beyond Selling: Use your platform to build a community and make a positive impact. Engaging with social issues and supporting causes can enhance brand loyalty and trust, particularly among younger consumers who value corporate social responsibility.
- Partnerships for a Cause: Consider partnerships with non-profit organizations or initiatives that align with your brand values to amplify your impact and reach.

CONCLUSION

The journey of digital marketing is one of discovery and innovation. Each step you take should aim not just at reaching more customers but at creating more meaningful engagements that build brand loyalty and drive conversions. The future of digital marketing holds boundless opportunities and challenges. By staying informed, embracing innovation, and adhering to a strategy that is flexible and forward-thinking, you can not only adapt to changes but also drive them. This proactive approach will ensure that your digital marketing efforts remain effective, relevant, and aligned with both business goals and the evolving digital landscape.

www.ingramcontent.com/pod-product-compliance
Lightning Source LLC
Chambersburg PA
CBHW071835210526
45479CB00001B/146